HNABU
HAUTANA · HAUTANA

Mythos Metropolis

Franziska Bollerey

Mythos Metropolis

Die Stadt als Sujet für Schriftsteller, Maler und Regisseure

The City as a Motif for Writers, Painters and Film Directors

GEBR. MANN VERLAG · BERLIN / IHAAU · TU DELFT

Gewidmet meiner Mutter, die mich das Hinschauen lehrte.

Mein Dank gilt Lida van Tongeren, für die freundschaftlich-verzahnte Ergänzung über so viele Jahre, Axel Föhl für dialogische Klärungen und Catharina van Esch für die souverän gehandhabte Positionierung von Texten und Bildern.

Inhalt

Contents

Editorische Notiz

Zwei Ansätze vereinigt der vorliegende Text: „Mythos Metropolis" vermittelt die Widerspiegelung der Metropole in Literatur, Film, Malerei und Grafik. „Europäische Metropolen im Wandel" analysiert Image, Gestaltung und Vermarktung von Städten seit dem 19. Jahrhundert.

„Mythos Metropolis" ist eine assoziative Reihung von Bildern und Texten als eine Seismographie von Impressionen, die die sensible, die künstlerische Psyche von den Reizungen der Großstadt empfängt. Modell waren hier die in eins gesetzten Bildskizzen- und Textspalten eines Filmdrehbuches als Versuch, Bild und Text so synchron wie irgend möglich miteinander zu verblenden.

In „Die sanfte Lesart" und „Die Masse montiert" nutzen Künste und Künstler die ihrem Metier je eigenen Mittel, das Phänomen Stadt zu interpretieren.

„Die Stadt als Bedrohung" und „Ich und die Stadt" zielen auf die Wahrnehmung des Kontrastes zwischen Sonnen- und Schattenseiten, zwischen Inferno und Erhabenheit des metropolitanen Lebens.

Schriftsteller, Maler und Filmregisseure kommen zu Wort in „Mythos Metropolis." Ihre Stimmen werden verwoben zu einer Textur von solchem Reichtum, wie ihn nur das komplexe Phänomen Metropolis hervorbringen konnte.

Der anschließende Essay „Europäische Metropolen im Wandel" objektiviert den Blick auf die Stadt und beschreibt die während fast zwei Jahrhunderten an Intensität zunehmenden Versuche zu ihrer Vermarktung. Er warnt vor einer Eindämpfung der im ersten Teil beschriebenen empfindlich-differenzierten Wahrnehmungen zu einem grob-griffigen „marketing image" der metropolitanen Stadt.

Sie könnte dazu führen, dass binnen kurzem der in „Mythos Metropolis" aufgefächerte Reichtum der Widerspiegelung städtischer Realität und Qualität unhinnehmbar reduziert werden würde. Preisgegeben würde damit die über Jahrhunderte akkumulierte, reiche Textur des Urbanen.

Mit Musils Zitat „wenn es Wirklichkeitssinn gibt... dann muss es auch etwas geben, das man Möglichkeitssinn nennen kann" wird der Leser aufgefordert, angeregt durch die Lektüre an einer Zukunft der Metropole mitzubauen, die es erlaubt, auch weiterhin von einem „Mythos Metropolis" zu sprechen und an ihm teilzuhaben.

Editorial Note

Two approaches are integrated into the present text: "Mythos Metropolis" conveys the mirror image of the metropolis in literature, film, painting and the graphic arts.
"The Changing face of the European Metropolis" analyses the image, shaping and marketing of cities since the 19th century.
"Mythos Metropolis" gives an associative stream of images and texts as a seismographic record of impressions, that the sensitive, the artist's psyche conceives of the stimulations of the big city. The integrated columns of pictorial sketches and texts in a filmscript served as a model for the attempt, to blend images and texts as intimately as possible.
In "The Gentle Way of Reading" and "A Montage of the Masses" arts and artists make use of the intrinsic means of their respective professions in interpreting the city as phenomenon.
"The City as a Threat" and "The City and I" aim for the perception of the contrast between sunny and shady side, between inferno and the sublime in metropolitan life.
Writers, painters and film directors are given a voice in "Mythos Metropolis." Their utterances are being interwoven into a texture of such richness, as can only be created by the complex phenomenon of the metropolis.

The following essay "The Changing Face of the European Metropolis" objectivizes the different views of the city and describes ever increasing attempts for its marketing over the last two centuries. It constitutes a warning against "down-boiling" all the sensitive-differentiated concepts of the city, whose development has been unfolded in the first part of the book, into a crude and catchy marketing image of the metropolis.
This process possibly might lead to an unbearable reduction of the wealth of mirror images of urban reality and quality as described in "Mythos Metropolis." The rich texture of urban life, accumulated over the centuries, would be given away in a very short time.
In the spirit of Musil's quotation "if there exists a sense for reality,... there also has to be a sense for possibility" the reader, animated by reading this book, is urged to take part in the construction of a metropolis, that also in the future allows to speak of a metropolitan mythos and even to take part in it.

Mythos Metropolis

Die Stadt als Sujet für Literaten, Künstler und Regisseure

The Myth of the Metropolis

The City as a Motif for Writers, Artists and Film Directors

Präambel

Es fiel mir nicht leicht, diesem Thema ein „Korsett" anzulegen. 1 Klar war von Anfang an, daß ich keine neuen Leitmotive kreieren wollte und auch nicht kann. 2 Aber dennoch: Stadtbild und Sinnbild: in wieviele Richtungen konnten die Gedanken da geschickt werden. Da gibt es die von André Corboz propagierte Bedeutungsforschung, 3 die mit Recht von der Städtebaugeschichte erwartet, das Wesen der Stadt nicht mehr als „Quantité négligeable" zu betrachten.[1] Keineswegs ist das „Invisible in Townplanning" belanglos - ganz gleich, ob man es rezipiert auf Plänen, 4-5 an Stadträumen oder in der Kunst untersuchen will. Stadtbild, Sinnbild, Bild: sind das überhaupt eindeutige Begriffe?

1 - Ruderer in Papier
1 - Rowing on a paper sea

2 - Zuschauer
2 - Spectators

Da gibt es das den Tatsachen entsprechende Bild von der Stadt als Megalopolis, 6-7 wie es das Nachrichtenmagazin *Time* in einer Titelgeschichte präsentiert: „Megacities. The world's sprawling urban centers are rife with problems and filled with promise... 8 By the millions they come, the ambitious and downtrodden of the world drawn by the strange magnetism of urban life. For centuries the progress of civilization has been defined by the inexorable growth of cities. Now the world is about to pass a milestone, more people will live in urban areas than in the countryside.

3 - Rom in Löwenform, 14. Jahrhundert
3 - Rome in the shape of a lion, 14th century

Preamble

It was not easy to wield this topic into a comprehensive form. 1
What I did know from the beginning was that I neither wanted to nor felt capable of creating a new leitmotif; 2 but even so, the terms *cityscape* and *symbol* send the mind in any number of directions. There is, for example, André Corboz's work of exegesis, 3 which quite rightly calls for the history of town planning to stop regarding the essential character of the city as a "quantité

4 - Piet Mondrian, Broadway Boogie Woogie, 1942/43
4 - Piet Mondrian, Broadway Boogie Woogie, 1942/43

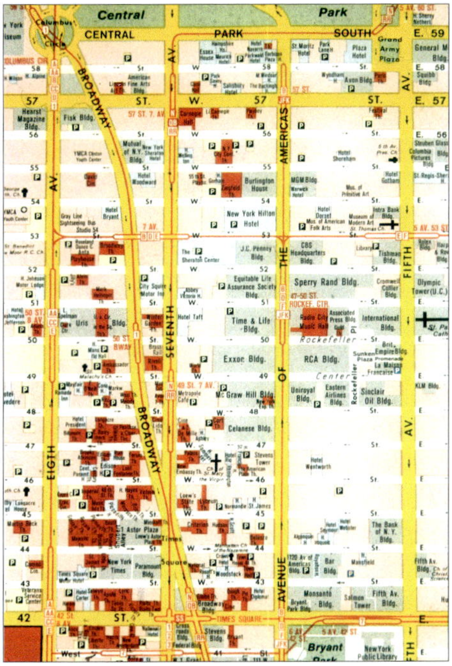

5 - Stadtplan New York, Theatre District, 2005
5 - New York City Map, Theatre District, 2005

négligeable".[1] The "invisible in town planning" is in no way irrelevant, regardless of whether one studies it in maps, 4-5 in the actual spaces of the city, or perceived through art. Cityscape (Stadtbild), Symbol (Sinnbild), Image (Bild): are these even defined terms? There is, for example, the factually anchored image of the city as megalopolis, 6-7 as presented in a cover story of the newsmagazine *Time*: "Megacities. The world's sprawling urban centres are rife with problems and filled with promise... 8 By the millions they come, the ambitious and the downtrodden of the world drawn by the strange magnetism of urban life. For centuries the progress of civilization has been defined by the inexorable growth of cities. Now the world is about to pass a milestone, more people will live in urban areas than in the countryside.

Does the growth of megacities portend an apocalypse of global epidemies and pollution? Or will the remarkable strength of selfreliance that can be found in some of them point the way to their salvation?“[2]
Hier wird die Anziehungskraft, der Magnetismus, den die Metropolen ausüben, genauso angesprochen wie die Bedrohung und die Gefahren, die sich in ihnen zusammenballen: „The bright sides and the dark sides of metropolis.“

Faszination und Elend, Apotheose und Apokalypse - das sind auch die Themen, an denen sich die Phantasie der Literaten, Künstler, Regisseure, Philosophen, Soziologen und Historiker immer wieder entzündet. Ich habe für meine Ausführungen keine systematische Gliederung gesucht, eher habe ich mich treiben lassen - nicht im Sinne eines „stream of consciousness“, sondern in Form einer assoziativen Mischung aus Entdeckung und Interpretation, die auf die unterschiedlichsten Kunstgattungen eingeht. Eine analytische Collage aus Zitaten, Interpretationen und Bildern.

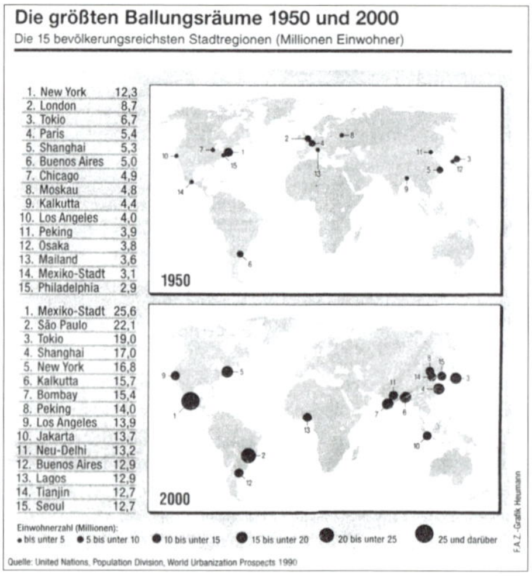

6 - Run auf Metropolen, Statistik 1990
6 - Run on the metropolises, statistics 1990

8 - "Time"- Titel: Megacities, 1993
8 - "Time" cover: Megacities, 1993

	1980		1990		2000		2010	
1	21.9	Tokyo	25.1	Tokyo	26.4	Tokyo	26.4	Tokyo
2	15.6	New York	16.1	New York	18.1	Mexico City	23.6	Bombay
3	13.9	Mexico City	15.1	Mexico City	18.1	Bombay	20.2	Lagos
4	12.5	Sao Paulo	15.1	Sao Paulo	17.8	Sao Paulo	19.7	Sao Paulo
5	11.7	Shangai	13.3	Shangai	16.6	New York	18.7	Mexico City
6	10.0	Osaka	12.2	Bombay	13.4	Lagos	18.4	Dhaka
7	9.9	Buenos Aires	11.5	Los Angeles	13.1	Los Angeles	17.2	New York
8	9.5	Los Angeles	11.2	Buenos Aires	12.9	Calcutta	16.6	Karachi
9	9.0	Calcutta	11.0	Osaka	12.9	Shangai	15.6	Calcutta
10	9.0	Beijing	10.9	Calcutta	12.6	Buenos Aires	15.3	Jakarta
11	8.9	Paris	10.8	Beijing	12.3	Dhaka	15.1	Delhi
12	8.7	Rio de Janeiro	10.5	Seoul	11.8	Karachi	13.9	Los Angeles
13	8.3	Seoul	9.7	Rio de Janeiro	11.7	Delhi	13.9	Metro Manila
14	8.1	Moscow	9.3	Paris	11.0	Jakarta	13.7	Buenos Aires
15	8.1	Bombay	9.0	Moscow	11.0	Osaka	13.7	Shangai
16	7.7	London	8.8	Tiajin	10.9	Metro Manila	12.7	Cairo
17	7.3	Tianjin	8.6	Cairo	10.8	Beijing	11.8	Istanbul
18	6.9	Cairo	8.2	Delhi	10.6	Rio de Janeiro	11.5	Beijing
19	6.8	Chicago	8.0	Metro Manila	10.6	Cairo	11.5	Rio de Janeiro
20	6.3	Essen	7.9	Karachi	9.9	Seoul	11.0	Osaka
21	6.0	Jakarta	7.7	Lagos	9.6	Paris	10.0	Tianjin
22	6.0	Metro Manila	7.7	London	9.5	Istanbul	9.9	Seoul
23	5.6	Delhi	7.7	Jakarta	9.3	Moscow	9.7	Paris
24	5.3	Milan	6.8	Chicago	9.2	Tianjin	9.4	Hyderabad
25	5.1	Teheran	6.6	Dhaka	7.6	London	9.4	Moscow
26	5.0	Karachi	6.5	Istanbul	7.4	Lima	9.0	Bangkok
27	4.7	Bangkok	6.4	Teheran	7.3	Bangkok	8.8	Lima
28	4.6	Saint Petersburg	6.4	Essen	7.2	Teheran	8.6	Lahore
29	4.6	Hong Kong	5.9	Bangkok	7.0	Chicago	8 2	Madras
30	4.4	Lima	5.8	Lima	6.9	Hong Kong	8.1	Teheran

7 - World Urbanization Prospects, UN 2004
7 - World Urbanization Prospects, UN 2004

Does the growth of megacities portend an apocalypse of global epidemics and pollution? Or will the remarkable strength of self-reliance that can be found in some of them point the way to their salvation?"[2] The quote thematises the attraction, the magnetism of large cities as well as the threat and the dangers tied up in them: "The bright sides and the dark sides of metropolis".

Fascination and misery, apotheosis and apocalypse, these are themes that, again and again, inspire the imagination of writers, artists, film directors, philosophers, sociologists and historians. I have sought no systematic structure for my presentation, but have rather permitted my thoughts to drift; not a stream of consciousness; rather an associative mixture of discovery and interpretation that involves all sorts of genres. An analytical collage, made up of quotations, interpretations and images.

Die sanfte Lesart

Stadtbild - Sinnbild: heißt das, der Stadt im Bildhaften einen Sinn verleihen oder mit 9-10 Symbolwerten hausieren gehen? Selbstverständlich hängt sowohl die Entschlüsselung der Bilder und Symbole als auch deren Verwertung von der Erwartungshaltung und vom Bewertungsstandpunkt des Rezipienten und/oder des Vermarkters ab. Augenscheinlich ist, daß es eine aggressive und eine sanfte Ausbeu-

9 - Werbeanzeige Yves Saint Laurent ‚Paris'
9 - Advertisement Yves Saint Laurent ‚Paris'

10 - Werbeanzeige Laura Biagiotti ‚Roma'
10 - Advertisement Laura Biagiotti ‚Roma'

tung von Bildern und Symbolen gibt. Die aggressive Haltung tritt dort zutage, wo die Stadt zu einer Ware degradiert und zu einer Ressource für Immobilienmakler, 11-12 Bauunternehmer und Spekulanten wird. *Die Stadt als Gabentisch*, wie Hans G. Helms[3] es ausdrückt. Demgegenüber gibt es die sanfte Ausbeutung durch die Sehmenschen. Als einen solchen bezeichnet sich George Grosz in seinen Briefen aus New York: „... ist eine dolle Sache. Ich meine für einen Sehmann. 13-14 Es sind einfach überwältigende Ansichten, von einer sonderbaren, fremden Buntheit, die fasziniert."[4]

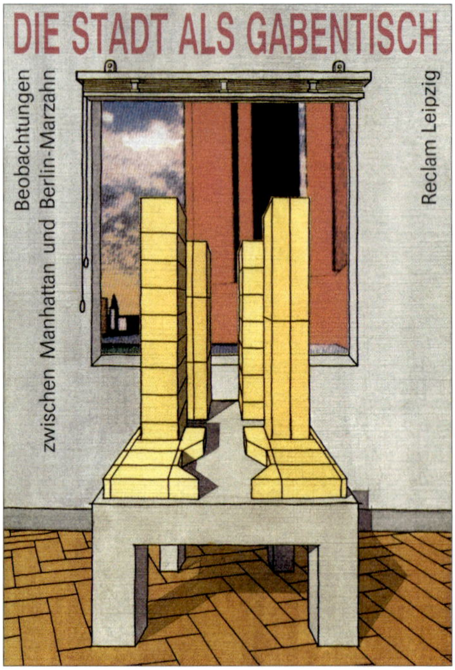

11 - Umschlag: Hans G. Helms (Hrsg.): „Die Stadt als Gabentisch"
11 - Cover: Hans.G. Helms (Ed.): "The City as a Table of Presents", 1992

The Gentle Way of Reading

Cityscape - symbol: does this mean giving importance to recognizable features of the city or 9-10 going around hawking symbolic values? Of course, both the deciphering of images and symbols and their exploitation depends on the attitude and the evaluative perspective of the perceiver and/or the seller. There is obviously an aggressive and a gentle exploitation of images and symbols. The aggressive attitude comes to light wherever the city is degraded to a commodity, to a resource for property dealers, 11-12 building contractors and speculators. *The city as a pile of wrapped gifts*, as Hans G. Helms[3] puts it. On the other hand we have the gentle exploitation of the "gazer". George Grosz qualifies himself as such in his letters from New York: "... it is a great thing. I mean for a gazer. 13-14 These sights are simply overpowering, fascinating in their strange and unusual colours."[4]

12 - Klaus Staeck, Eigentum verpflichtet zur Ausbeutung, Fotomontage, 1973
12 - Klaus Staeck, Property Obliges to Exploit, photomontage, 1973

13 - Umschlag 1985: George Grosz: „Memories of New York", 1917
13 - Cover 1985: George Grosz: "Memories of New York", 1917

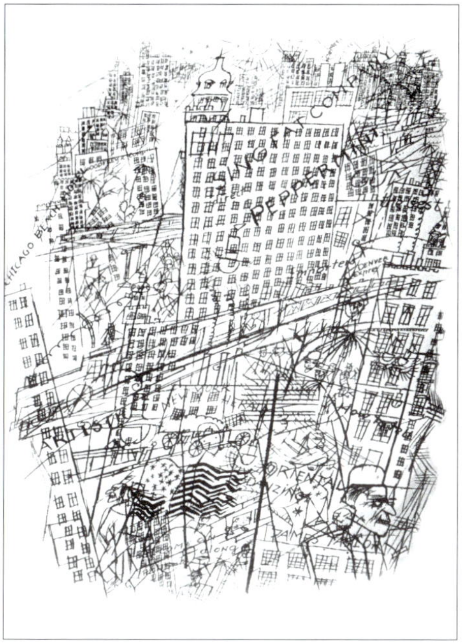

14 - George Grosz, Erinnerung an New York, Lithographie, 1915/16
14 - George Grosz, Memories of New York, lithograph, 1915/16

Die Sehmenschen lassen, indem sie die Städte mit ihren jeweiligen Mitteln abbilden, diese über sich selbst reden, ohne sie zu vergewaltigen. Ihre „Realität aus zweiter Hand" - die der Sehmenschen - tritt an, um Emotionen, Assoziationen, Phantasien zu wecken. 15-16 Ihre Wahrnehmung des Stadtbildes provoziert die Schöpfung neuer Bilder. Das Affirmative muß ihnen fremd sein, denn es verschließt den Deutungen und Interpretationen die Tür. Und gerade sie sind das Material, aus dem die Filme, Gemälde, Romane und Gedichte sind. Die sanfte Ausbeutung steht somit der aggressiven Ausbeutung kontrapunktisch gegenüber. Dies spricht Wim Wenders in einer vorsichtigen Mahnung 1991 in seinem Referat „The Urban Landscape" vor japanischen Architekten aus: „Ich bitte Sie, Ihre Arbeit für einen Moment anders zu betrachten, als Aufgabe, künftigen Kindern Herkunftsorte zu schaffen, Städte und Landschaften, die die Bilderwelt und die Vorstellungskraft dieser Kinder formen werden. Und ich möchte, daß Sie das Gegenteil dessen in Erwägung ziehen, was per Definition Ihre Aufgabe ist: nicht nur Gebäude zu konstruieren, sondern Freiräume zu schaffen, um Leere zu bewahren, damit das VOLLE nicht unsere Sicht versperrt und das Leere zum Ausruhen erhalten bleibt."[5]

Ähnlich wie Sten Nadolny in seiner *Entdeckung der Langsamkeit*[6] der Schnelligkeit, dem sogenannten effizienten Umgang mit der Zeit, den Krieg erklärt, plädiert Wim Wenders für Stillstand; das heißt: nicht Stadtreparatur um jeden Preis. Nicht die affirmative, sondern die kontemplative Planung entspricht seinem Wunschbild von der Stadt. Es muß Raum geben für Pausen, Pausen zum optischen Luftholen, zur Besinnung, zur Sinngebung, zur Verdauung, zur Anregung.
„Städte erzählen keine Geschichten. Aber sie können etwas über GESCHICHTE erzählen. Städte können ihre Geschichte in sich tragen 17-18 und können sie zeigen, sie können sie sichtbar machen, oder sie können sich verbergen. Sie können Augen öffnen, so wie Filme, oder sie können sie schließen,"[7] so Wim Wenders.

15 - Berlin-Prenzlauer Berg, Sockelzone, 1987
15 - Berlin-Prenzlauer Berg, Building´s base, 1987

16 - Berlin-Prenzlauer Berg, Sockelzone, 1987
16 - Berlin-Prenzlauer Berg, Building´s base, 1987

17 - Berlin-Prenzlauer Berg, „Zur gemütlichen Ecke“, 1986
17 - Berlin-Prenzlauer Berg, "Cozy Corner", 1986

18 - Berlin-Schöneberg, ehemalige Poliklinik der Reichsbahn, 1989
18 - Berlin-Schöneberg, former outpatients clinic of Reichsbahn, 1989

By depicting cities in their different media these "gazers" allow cities to speak for themselves without violating them. Their "second-hand reality" has the purpose of stirring emotions, associations, fantasies. 15-16 Their perception of the cityscape triggers the creation of new images. The affirmative must be alien to them, since it closes the door on understanding and interpretation. And these are precisely what constitute the material of films, paintings, novels and poems. Gentle exploitation is the polar opposite of aggressive exploitation. This is what Wim Wenders gives voice to in the cautious warning that ends his paper *The Urban Landscape* presented to Japanese architects in Tokyo in 1991: "I ask you to view your work differently for just one moment, as an exercise in providing future children with a place of origin, cities and landscapes that will form the visual world and imaginative powers of these children.
And I want you to consider the opposite of what is by definition your work: not only the construction of buildings, but the creation of spaces. We must avoid cluttering our view and preserve emptiness as space for respite."[5]
Like Sten Nadolny, who declares war on speed - the so-called efficient relation to time - in his *Die Entdeckung der Langsamkeit*[6] (The Discovery of Slowness), Wim Wenders pleads for stasis rather than city repair at any price. Contemplative rather than affirmative planning correlates with his ideal vision of the city. There must be room for pauses, pauses for an optical breather, for reflection, for making sense, for digestion, for stimulation.

"Cities do not tell a story. But they can tell us a lot about HISTORY. Cities can carry their history in themselves 17-18 and they can show it, they can make it visual, or they can hide it. They can open eyes, just as films can, or they can close them. They can speak out, or they can nurture the imagination,"[7] according to Wim Wenders.

„In Berlin, wo ich lebe, ermöglichen es diese leeren Räume den Menschen, das Stadt-Bild zu durchschauen. Nicht nur im Sinne von: eine Fläche zu überschauen (vielleicht sogar bis zum Horizont, was auf jeden Fall eine angenehme Erfahrung in einer Stadt ist), sondern sie können durch diese Lücken hindurch etwas sehen im Sinne von: die Zeit überschauen."[8]
Und er fährt fort: „Wir müssen für all das Kleine kämpfen, das es noch gibt. Das Kleine verleiht dem Großen einen Blickwinkel. 19-20
In der Geschichte des Kinos waren die kleinen Filme die Wiege der Kreativität, neuer Ideen, kühner Inhalte, menschlicher und warmer und wahrhafter Geschichten. Die kleinen Filme waren Reservoirs des Denkens.
In einer Stadt sind das Kleine, das Leere, das Offene die Batterien, die es uns erlauben, aufzutanken, die uns gegen die Übermacht des Großen beschützen."[9]
Wenders' Film *Der Himmel über Berlin* (1987) wäre nicht denkbar ohne die Bedeutungskraft der Leere. 21-22

19 - Berlin-Kreuzberg, Firmenreklame, 1980er Jahre
19 - Berlin-Kreuzberg, Commercial advertisement, 1980ies

21 - Berlin-Kreuzberg, Lindenstraße, 1970er Jahre
21 - Berlin-Kreuzberg, Lindenstraße, 1970ies

Ruinengrundstücke: Es gab keine besseren „Abenteuerspielplätze" im Nachkriegsberlin. 23-24 Und heute? Der Kriegsschutt ist lange weggeräumt und in den westlichen Innenstadtbezirken sind die Baulücken nahezu restlos gefüllt, die Brandmauern unsichtbar, die Geschichte zubetoniert.

23 - Friedrich Seidenstücker, Ruinen - „Ihr Schneider", nach 1945
23 - Friedrich Seidenstücker, Ruins - "Your Taylor", after 1945

20 - Berlin-Mitte, Brandmauer, 1980er Jahre
20 - Berlin-Mitte, Advertisement on fire wall, 1980ies

22 - Berlin-Kreuzberg, Lindenstraße, 1970er Jahre
22 - Berlin-Kreuzberg, Lindenstraße, 1970ies

24 - Henry Ries, Berlin, „Das Leben geht weiter", 1948
24 - Henry Ries, "Life goes on", 1948

"In Berlin, where I live, these empty spaces allow people to look through the cityscape, the image of the city. Not just in the sense of looking out over a plain (perhaps even to the horizon, which is in any case an agreeable experience in the city), but they can see something else through these gaps: they can look out over time."[8]
And he continues: "We must fight to preserve everything small that still remains. The small puts the big into perspective. 19-20
In the history of the cinema the small films were the cradles of creativity, of new ideas, daring content, stories that were more human and warmer and truer. The small films were the reservoirs of thought. In a city, the small, the empty and the open are the batteries that allow us to recharge, that protect us from the overpowering influence of the big."[9]
Wenders' film *Wings of Desire* (1987) would have been unthinkable without the significance of space. 21-22

War ruins: there were no better "adventure playgrounds" in post-war Berlin. 23-24 And today; the rubble of war has long been cleared away and the gaps in the western inner city districts have been filled, the "fire-walls" rendered invisible, history sealed away under concrete.

Diesem Schicksal entkommen auch die größeren Brachen im Zentrum diesseits und jenseits der ehemaligen Mauer nicht. 25-26 Heidi Lüdi, die Szenographin des Wenders-Films wird dann nicht mehr auf der Suche nach dem geeigneten Stadtbild ihrer Begeisterung über den Stadtrand-Charakter im geographischen Herzen der ehemaligen Doppelstadt Ausdruck verleihen können:

„Hier gewinnt die Stadtbrache Bedeutung. Die Leere, die offenen Flächen, der Horizont schafft das Gefühl eines zeitlosen, eines freien Raumes. Hier ist das beruhigend Nutzlose, der noch nicht durch aggressive Ausbeutung kommerzialisierte Ort.“[10]

Folgerichtig wich Wim Wenders auf der Suche nach dem geeigneten Stadtbild an den tatsächlichen Stadtrand (die Ästhetik der Peripherie, wie sie Pier Paolo Pasolini oder später auch Ettore Scola fasziniert hat) aus in die Industriebrachen von Hennigsdorf, Rüdersdorf oder Oranienburg.

25 - Berlin-Kreuzberg, Brandmauern in der Lindenstraße, 1970er Jahre
25 - Berlin-Kreuzberg, Lindenstraße, Fire walls, 1970ies

The larger wastelands in the centre on both sides of the former Wall will hardly escape this fate. 25-26 And Heidi Lüdi, the scenographer of Wenders' film, on the lookout for suitable cityscapes, will no longer be able to give expression to her enthusiasm for the outskirts-feel in the geographic heart of the former double-city:
"Here the urban wasteland gains meaning. The emptiness, the open spaces, the horizon create the feeling of a timeless, free space. There is a calming uselessness here, a place that has yet to be commercialized by aggressive exploitation."[10]
Consequently, Wenders soon extended his search for suitable cityscapes to the real outskirts (the "aesthetic of the periphery," that fascinated Pier Paolo Pasolini and later Ettore Scola) and went to the industrial wastelands of Hennigsdorf, Rüdersdorf or Oranienburg.

26 - Berlin-Kreuzberg, Brandmauern in der Lindenstraße, 1970er Jahre
26 - Berlin-Kreuzberg, Lindenstraße, Fire walls, 1970ies

27 - Berlin-Moabit, Hinterhöfe in der Lehrter Straße, 1983
27 - Berlin-Moabit, Lehrter Straße, Backyards, 1983

29 - Berlin-Wedding, Brandmauer in der Groninger Straße, 1982
29 - Berlin-Wedding, Groninger Straße, Fire Wall, 1982

Ich möchte noch einmal Wim Wenders zu Wort kommen lassen:
„Als ich *Der Himmel über Berlin* drehte, bemerkte ich, daß ich stets diese leeren Flächen suchte, diese Niemandsländer. Ich hatte das Gefühl, diese Stadt kann sich viel besser durch ihre leeren Stellen definieren als durch ihre vollen... Berlin hat viele leere Flächen. 27-28 Man sieht Häuser, die auf einer Seite komplett frei sind, weil das Nachbarhaus zerstört und nicht wieder aufgebaut wurde. Die trostlosen Seitenwände solcher Häuser nennt man Brandmauern, 29-30 und man sieht sie kaum in anderen Städten. Diese leeren Flächen sind die Wunden, und ich mag die Stadt aufgrund ihrer Wunden. Sie vermitteln Geschichte besser als jedes Geschichtsbuch oder Dokument."[11]

28 - Alfred Pfitzner, Berliner Hinterhäuser im Schnee, 1930
28 - Alfred Pfitzner, Houses at the Back in Snow, 1930

It seems fitting to use Wenders' words again:
"When I was shooting *Wings of Desire*, I noticed that I was constantly looking for these open expanses, these no man's lands. I felt that this city could define itself much better through its empty places than through its full ones... Berlin has many open spaces. 27-28 There are houses that are completely exposed on one side because the neighbouring building was destroyed and never rebuilt. The desolate side walls of such houses are called 'fire-walls' (Brandmauern), 29-30 and they are rarely found in other cities. These empty surfaces are wounds, and I like the city for its wounds. They communicate history better than any history book or document."[11]

30 - Berlin-Wilmersdorf, Brandmauer in der Düsseldorfer Straße, 1980er Jahre
30 - Berlin-Wilmersdorf, Düsseldorfer Straße, Fire Wall, 1980ies

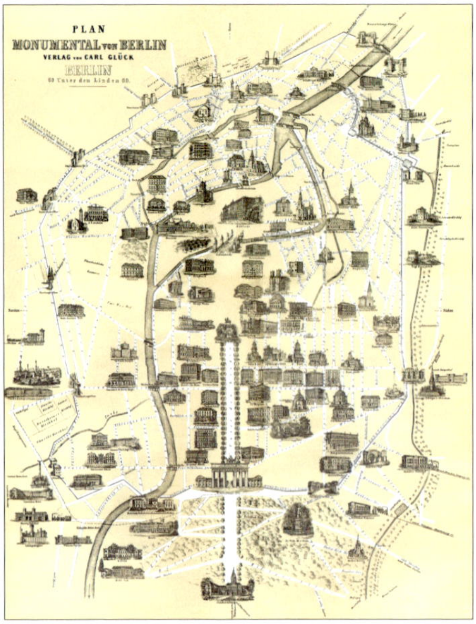

31 - Carl Glück, Plan Monumental von Berlin, 1860
31 - Carl Glück, "Monumental Plan of Berlin", 1860

Und an anderer Stelle heißt es: „Ich bin sicher, daß diese Brandwände einen viel stärkeren Erinnerungswert haben als die bemalten Fassaden. Und, ja, das ‚Kaputte' gräbt sich sicher deutlicher in die Erinnerung ein als das ‚Heile'. Das ‚Kaputte' hat sozusagen eine griffigere Oberfläche, an der sich die Erinnerung festhalten kann. An all den sauberen Flächen des ‚Heilen' rutscht die Erinnerung ab."[12]

Hier wird ein Stadtbild beschrieben, das seine Bedeutung nicht aus der Vielzahl von Monumenten bezieht 31-32 oder dem einen unverwechselbaren Monument, welches gleichsam zum Symbol für die Gesamtstadt avanciert ist, 33-34 sondern ein Bild als Leseübung: „Die Mauer, die erzählt."

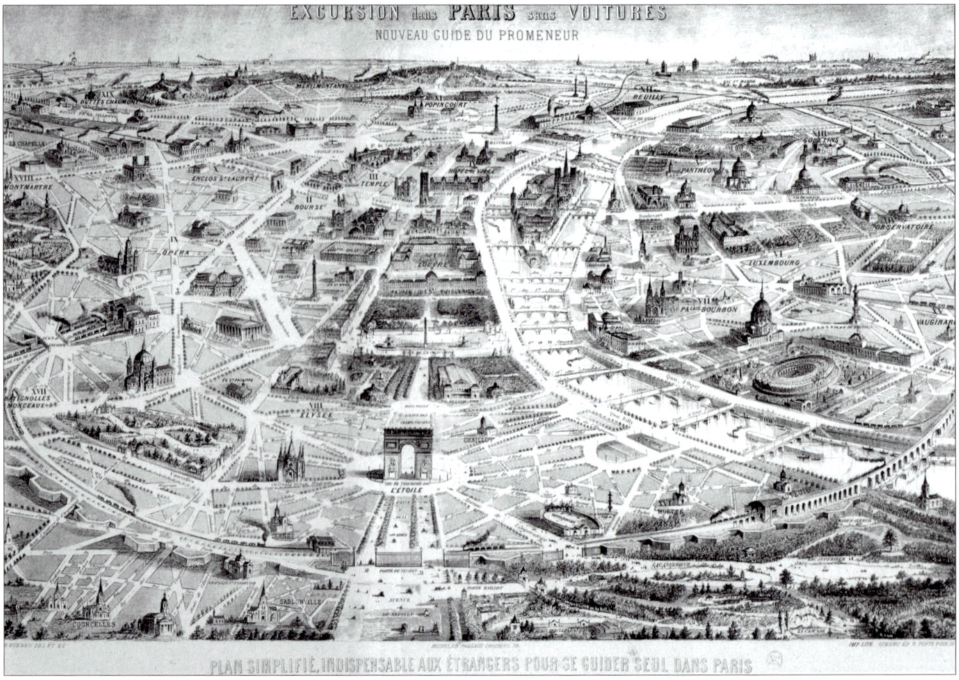

32 - H. Guesnu, Plan simplifié Paris, um 1867
32 - H.Guesnu, Simplified Plan of Paris, ca.1867

33 - Johannes Grützke, Berlin, 1985
33 - Johannes Grützke, Berlin, 1985

On another occasion he remarks: "I am sure that these fire-walls have a much stronger effect on memory than the painted façades. The 'broken' engraves itself on the mind much more clearly than the 'intact'.
In a manner of speaking the 'broken' supplies surfaces where memory can take hold. Memory slides off the clean surfaces of the 'intact'."[12]

Here we are dealing with a cityscape whose meaning is nurtured not merely by its many monuments, 31-32 or by its one unmistakable monument, 33-34 but rather by an image that is an exercise in reading: "The wall that speaks."

34 - Gilbert Legrand, Vergeßt Paris nicht
34 - Gilbert Legrand, Don't forget Paris

(...) Es war in jedem Streifen, der abgeschunden war, es war in den feuchten Blasen am unteren Rande der Tapeten, es schwankte in den abgerissenen Fetzen, und aus den garstigen Flecken, die vor langer Zeit entstanden waren, schwitzte es aus. Und aus diesen blau, grün und gelb gewesenen Wänden, die eingerahmt waren von den Bruchbahnen der zerstörten Zwischenmauern, stand die Luft dieser Leben heraus, die zähe, träge, stockige Luft, die kein Wind noch zerstreut hatte. (...)

35 - Abrißwand im Quartier Goutte d'Or, Paris, 1990
35 - Wall next to a demolished house in Goutte d'Or quarter, Paris, 1990

„Ich weiß nicht, ob ich schon gesagt habe, daß ich diese Mauer meine,“ 35 schreibt Rainer Maria Rilke in den *Aufzeichnungen des Malte Laurids Brigge*:
„Man sah ihre Innenseite. Man sah in den verschiedenen Stockwerken Zimmerwände, an denen noch die Tapeten klebten, da und dort den Ansatz des Fußbodens oder der Decke. Neben den Zimmerwänden blieb die ganze Mauer entlang noch ein schmutzigweißer Raum, und durch diesen kroch in unsäglich widerlichen, wurmweichen, gleichsam verdauenden Bewegungen die offene, rostfleckige Rinne der Abortröhre. Von den Wegen, die das Leuchtgas gegangen war, waren graue, staubige Spuren am Rande der Decken geblieben, und sie bogen da und dort, ganz unerwartet, rund um und kamen in die farbige Wand hineingelaufen und in ein Loch hinein, das schwarz und rücksichtslos ausgerissen war. Am unvergeßlichsten aber waren die Wände selbst. Das zähe Leben dieser Zimmer hatte sich nicht zertreten lassen. Es war noch da, es hielt sich an den Nägeln, die geblieben waren, es stand auf dem handbreiten Rest der Fußböden, es war unter den Ansätzen der Ecken, wo es noch ein klein wenig Innenraum gab, zusammengekrochen. Man konnte sehen, daß es in der Farbe war, die es langsam, Jahr um Jahr, verwandelt hatte: Blau in schimmliges Grün, Grün in Grau und Gelb in ein altes, abgestandenes Weiß, das fault. Aber es war auch in den frischeren Stellen, die sich hinter Spiegeln, Bildern und Schränken erhalten hatten; denn es hatte ihre Umrisse gezogen und nachgezogen und war mit Spinnen und Staub auch auf diesen versteckten Plätzen gewesen, die jetzt bloßlagen. Es war in jedem Streifen, der abgeschunden war, es war in den feuchten Blasen am unteren Rande der Tapeten, es schwankte in den abgerissenen Fetzen, und aus den garstigen Flecken, die vor langer Zeit entstanden waren, schwitzte es aus. Und aus diesen blau, grün und gelb gewesenen Wänden, die eingerahmt waren von den Bruchbahnen der zerstörten Zwischenmauern, stand die Luft dieser Leben heraus, die zähe, träge, stockige Luft, die kein Wind noch zerstreut hatte. Da standen die Mittage und die Krankheiten und das Ausgeatmete und der jahrealte Rauch und der Schweiß, der unter den Schultern ausbricht und die Kleider schwer macht, und das Fade aus den Munden und der Fuselgeruch gärender Füße. Da stand das Scharfe vom Urin und das Brennen vom Ruß und grauer Kartoffeldunst und der schwere, glatte Gestank von alterndem Schmalze. Der süße, lange Geruch von vernachlässigten Säuglingen war da und der Angstgeruch der Kinder, die in die Schule gehen, und das Schwüle aus den Betten mannbarer Knaben. Und vieles hatte sich dazu gesellt, was von unten gekommen war, aus dem Abgrund der Gasse, die verdunstete, und anderes war von oben herabgesickert mit dem Regen, der über den Städten nicht rein ist. Und manches hatten die schwachen, zahm gewordenen Hauswinde, die immer in derselben Straße bleiben, zugetragen, und es war noch vieles da, wovon man den Ursprung nicht wußte. Ich habe doch gesagt, daß man alle Mauern abgebrochen hatte bis auf die letzte - ? Nun von dieser Mauer spreche ich fortwährend.“[13]

Kurt Tucholsky faßt dieses Bild Rilkes, den Atem der Mauern und Häuser ebenfalls für seine Phantasie ausbeutend, in seinem Gedicht *Häuser* zusammen:

„Mittleres Haus in der Köpenicker Strasse, in der Avenue des Ternes,
am Harvestehuderweg -
du bist vollgelebt.

Hinter deinen Tapeten hat sich Angelebtes versammelt,
nachts knistert es,
tagsüber dünsten dort hundert Leben aus,
mittleres Haus...“[14]

"I do not know whether I have already said that it is this wall I mean," 35 writes Rainer Maria Rilke in *The Notebooks of Malte Laurids Brigge*:
"One saw its inner side. One saw, at the different storeys, the walls of the rooms to which the paper still clung, and here and there marks of the beams of flooring or ceiling. Near the room partitions there still remained, along the whole length of the wall, a greyish-white streak; across this there crept in worm-like spirals that seemed to serve some unspeakably disgusting digestive function, the gaping, rust-covered channel of the water-closet pipe. At the ceiling edges remained grey, dusty traces of the paths the gas-pipes had followed; they bent hither and thither, taking unexpected turns, and ran along the painted walls into a black hole that had been carelessly torn out. But the walls themselves were the most unforgettable. The stubborn life of these rooms had not allowed itself to be trampled out. It was still there; it clung to the nails that had been left in the walls; it found a resting-place on the remaining handsbreadth of flooring; it squatted beneath the corner beams where a little bit of space remained. One could see it in the colours which it had slowly changed, year by year: blue into a mouldy green, green into grey, and yellow into a stale, drab, weary white. But it was also in the places that had kept fresher, behind the mirrors, the pictures, and the wardrobes; for it had outlined their contours over and over again, and had been with cobwebs and dust even in these hidden retreats that now lay uncovered. It was in every bare, flayed streak of surface, it was in the blisters the dampness had raised at the edges of the wall-papers; it floated in the torn-off shreds, and sweated out of the long-standing spots of filth. And from these walls once blue, and green and yellow, framed by the tracks of the disturbed partitions, the breath of these lives came forth the clammy, sluggish, fusty breath, which no wind had yet scattered. There were the midday meals and the sicknesses and the exhalations and the smoke of years, and the sweat that breaks out under the armpits and makes the garments heavy, and the stale breath of mouths, and the oily odour of perspiring feet. There were the pungent tang of urine and the stench of burning soot and the grey reek of potatoes, and the heavy, sickly fumes of rancid grease. The sweetish, lingering smell of neglected infants was there, and the smell of frightened children who go to school, and the stuffiness of the beds of nubile youths. To these was added much that had risen from the pit of the reeking street below, and more that had oozed down from above with the rain, which over cities is not clean. And much the feeble, tamed, domestic winds, that always stay in the same street, had borne thither; and much more was there, the sources of which were not known. I said, did I not, that all the walls had been demolished except the last ? It is of this wall I have been speaking all along."[13]

Kurt Tucholsky concentrated Rilke's image, also imaginatively exploiting the idea of the breath of walls and houses, for his poem *Häuser* (Houses):

"Middle-class house
on Köpenickerstrasse,
On the Avenue des
Ternes,
on Harvestehuderweg -
You have been lived to
the full.

Behind your wallpaper
something has col-
lected and stuck,
And at night it rustles,
Hundreds of lives
evaporate there every
day,
Middle-class house..."[14]

Die Masse montiert

Neben dieser Stadt der sanften Lesart, gibt es das Porträt der lauten, sich aufdrängenden Stadt: die Stadt der Quantitäten, der Schnelligkeit, der Überheblichkeit, des Lärms, des Lichts, der schrillen Töne, der konkurrierenden Bilder und Zeichen. 36 Michel Butor z.B. spricht von der „Stadt als Anhäufung von Text“:
„In manchen großen Straßen häufen sich riesige, prunkende, leuchtende, blinkende, wechselnde Aufschriften, dies oder jenes in bekannten oder unbekannten, hellen oder dunklen Buchstaben anpreisend. In den Schaufenstern geben Schildchen die Preise an, präzisieren Qualität und Herkunft der Waren; in den Restaurants Speisekarten; in den Museen mitunter lange Kommentare. Wo ich auch halt mache, bin ich umgeben, eingekreist von Text, 37 und beim Zurechtfinden innerhalb dieser Masse können bestimmte Bücher mir helfen, solche, die mir eine Analyse der äußeren Beschaffenheit dieses Ensembles geben, oft mit Hilfe von Karten, Plänen, Übersichten, und es mir ermöglichen, am Verkehr teilzunehmen, mich von einem Anhaltspunkt zum anderen zu bewegen: ich weiß dann, welches Viertel ein bestimmter Name meint, welcher Art es ist, welche Möglichkeiten es bietet, welche besonderen Merkmale und welche auffälligen Punkte.“[15]

36 - George Grosz, Die Großstadt, 1916/1917
36 - George Grosz, Big City, 1916/17

A Montage of the Masses

This city seen through the gentle way of reading is not the only one, however. It coexists with the portrait of the loud, obtrusive city: the city of quantities, of speed, of meaninglessness, of noise, of light, of piercing sounds, of competing images and signs. 36 Michel Butor, for example, speaks of the "city as an accumulation of text": "Huge, showy, dazzling, flashing signs praising this or that in familiar or unfamiliar, bright or dark letter accumulate in some large streets. Small labels in shop windows advertise prices, quality and origins of the goods; there are menus in restaurants; there are long commentaries in museums. Wherever I stop I find myself surrounded and enclosed by text, 37 and certain books can aid my orientation within these masses, books that give me an analysis of the outer qualities of the whole, often with the aid of maps, plans and surveys; these allow me to become part of the traffic, to move from one focal point to another: I then know which area is meant by a particular name, what it is like, the possibilities it offers, its special features and sights."[15]

37 - Christa Dichgans, Erinnerungen an New York, 1981
37 - Christa Dichgans, N.Y. Memories, 1981

„Picadilly Circus", „Times Square" und - als pars pro toto der geballten Zeichen - Tokyo: 38 so schreit sich die Stadt des 20. und 21. Jahrhunderts ins Bewußtsein des Städters.
„Und so wie die uns umgebende Bilderwelt immer kakophonischer, disharmonischer, lauter, vielgestaltiger und angeberischer wird, so werden die Städte komplexer, mißtönender, lauter, unübersichtlicher und überwältigender. Sie passen gut zusammen, die Städte und die Bilder. Betrachten Sie nur diese alles überschwemmende Anzahl von Stadt-Bildern: die Verkehrsschilder, die riesigen Neonschriften auf den Dächern, die Reklametafeln und Poster, die Schaufenster, die Videowände, die Zeitungsstände, die Verkaufsautomaten, die ‚Botschaften' auf Autos, LKWs und Bussen, all die bildlichen Informationen in Taxen oder U-Bahnen; jede Plastiktüte ist mit irgendwas bedruckt 39-40 etc. etc.,"[16] konstatiert Wim Wenders.

38 - Lichtreklame, Tokio, 1994
38 - Neon advertisement, Tokyo, 1994

"Picadilly Circus", "Times Square" and the crowded signs of Tokyo 38 are the pars pro toto, the way in which the city of the 20th and 21st century forces itself into the consciousness of the inhabitant.
"Just as the pictorial world which surrounds us becomes ever more cacophonic, disharmonious, louder, multiform and showy, so too the cities become more complex, dissonant, louder, complicated and overwhelming. Images and cities go well together. Just look at this overwhelming number of city images: traffic signs, huge neon signs on rooftops, the billboards and posters, the shop windows, the video walls, the newspaper stands, the vending machines, the 'messages' on cars, trucks and busses, all the visual information in taxis and subways: every plastic bag has something printed on it, 39-40 etc. etc.,"[16] states Wenders.

39 - Plastiktüte „Elbeo", 1980
39 - Plastic bag "Elbeo", 1980

40 - Plastiktüte „New Yorker", 1991
40 - Plastic bag "New Yorker", 1991

41 - Nikolaus Braun, Berliner Straßenzene, 1921
41 - Nikolaus Braun, Berlin Street Scene, 1921

Masse, Häufung, Schnelligkeit, Inkongruenz, Simultaneität, Dichte, Chaos: dies alles sind substantivische Charakterisierungen der großen Stadt. Sie waren schon immer der provokative Nährboden für Künstler und Literaten, sie waren der Anlaß zur Schaffung immer wieder neuer Stadtbilder: 41 Masse Mensch, Masse Stein, Masse Bild, Masse Geräusch, Masse Licht, Masse Atmosphäre und ihre Domestizierung mit dem Mittel der Collage und der Montage.

Bereits Giovanni Battista Piranesi hat ab 1740 ein künstlerisches Mittel, eine Methode der Darstellung gesucht, um der Überlagerungen, den Simultaneitäten, der Masse und Dichte Herr zu werden. Seine *Antichità Romane*, 42 seine *Carceri* sind ein Ausdruck der Vernetzung des Nebeneinanders von Stein, Geschichte und Leben. Sie sind Versuche zur Eroberung des Labyrinthes Stadt. Über das collagierende Verweben hinaus geht Piranesi in seinem *Pianta di Roma*, dem berühmten Marmorplan und seinen Stichen zum *Campo Marzio*. 43 Hier montiert er die Bauten des antiken Rom zu idealen Stadträumen einer neuen Metropole.[17]

42 - Giovanni Battista Piranesi, Idea della antiche (Vision der alten) Via Appia e Ardeatina, 1757
42 - Giovanni Battista Piranesi, Ideal view of the ancient Via Appia and Ardeatina, 1757

43 - Giovanni Battista Piranesi, Pianta di Roma (Plan von Rom), 1756
43 - Giovanni Battista Piranesi, Map of Rome, 1756

Masses, accumulation, speed, incongruence, simultaneity, density, chaos: these are all nouns describing the large city. They have always provided a stimulating and fertile soil for artists and writers; they inspired the creation of ever newer cityscapes. 41 Masses of people, of stone, of images, of noise, of light, and of atmosphere, and their domestication by the means of collage or montage.

As far back as 1740 Giovanni Battista Piranesi had already searched for an artistic medium, a method of representation that would dominate these superimpositions, the simultaneity, mass and density. His *Antichità di Roma*, 42 his *Carceri* are an expression of the entwinement of stone, history and life coexisting alongside one another. They are attempts to conquer the labyrinth of the city. In his engravings of the *Campo Marzio* Piranesi goes beyond a collage-like interweaving. 43 He assembles the edifices of ancient Rome to create ideal cityscapes of a new metropolis.[17]

Knapp zweihundert Jahre später wird die Montage zum künstlerischen Mittel par excellence für den Aufbau von Filmen aus einzelnen Bild- und Handlungseinheiten.

Ein anderes, ebenso modernes Mittel zur Charakterisierung der Metropole Paris wählt der Literat Louis-Sébastien Mercier in seinem zwischen 1781 und 1788 erschienenen *Tableau de Paris*.[18] 44-45 Wie ein Beleuchter läßt er seine Schlaglichter über die Stadt streichen und bündelt sie zu immer wieder neuen Reportagen. Von unersättlicher Neugier getrieben, ist er tage- und nächtelang unterwegs. Kritiker sprechen von „mit den Beinen geschriebenen Berichten" seiner Wanderungen in der Großstadt. - Ein Flaneur, wie wir ihm u.a. in Charles Baudelaire und Walter Benjamin später wiederbegegnen oder wie er dem Werk von György Konrád inhärent ist, der Wien und Budapest als „spazierliche" Metropolen porträtiert.[19]

44 - Porträt von Louis-Sébastien Mercier, Stahlstich von Torchiana
44 - Portrait of Louis-Sébastien Mercier, steel-plate engraving by Torchiana

Noch unter einem anderen Aspekt betrachtet war Mercier modern. Er studierte Paris bis in seine letzten Winkel und bis zu den Ärmsten und Verkommensten seiner Einwohner. Er schrieb mit größter Aufmerksamkeit und Beobachtungsgabe über Gefängnisse, Makler, Armenkrankenhäuser, Verleger, Dirnen und Zuhälter, Ärzte, Kammerzofen, Taschendiebe, Müßiggänger, Kaffeehäuser und öffentliche Abtritte. Hier ein Beleg: „Dieweil es in Paris keine öffentlichen Latrinen gibt, werden Quais und Promenaden dazu gemacht. Sollten Tabakhändler und Parfümfabrikanten der Grund dafür sein, daß die Polizei gegen derlei Unschicklichkeit noch nicht vorgegangen ist? Jene Leute, die so oft gegen den einen oder anderen Mißstand wettern, sollten sie nicht einmal Eifer auf die Anstößigkeit wenden, die darin liegt, daß ein Mann mitten auf der Straße oder an einem Eckstein seine Hosen herunterläßt? Es scheint, sie warten, bis die Frauen sich die gleiche Freiheit nehmen; dann werden sie zwei Fliegen mit einer Klappe schlagen."[20]

Nearly two hundred years later the montage became the artistic medium par excellence for the making of films out of single images and action segments.

The writer Louis-Sébastien Mercier chose an equally modern medium to characterize the metropolis of Paris in his *Tableau de Paris*,[18] which appeared between 1781 and 1788. 44-45 Like a lighting technician, he allows beams of light to glide over the city, assembling material for more and more articles. Driven by an insatiable curiosity, he roamed through the city day and night. Critics speak of "reports written with his legs" when referring to his wanderings through the great city. He was a flaneur like Charles Baudelaire or Walter Benjamin in later years, and he is inherent in the work of György Konrád, who portrayed Vienna and Budapest as "strolling" metropolises.[19]

Mercier was modern from another point of view as well. He studied Paris right down to the last nook and cranny, to the poorest and most wretched of its inhabitants. He wrote with the greatest focus and perception about prisoners, dealers, pauper's hospitals, publishers, prostitutes and pimps, doctors, lady's maids, pickpockets, idlers, coffee houses and public toilets. Here is one example: "As there are no public latrines in Paris, quays and promenades are used as such. Is it perhaps the fault of tobacconists and perfume manufacturers that the police have as yet made no move on such indecency? Those who so often rage over this or that grievance, should they not turn their energies to the offence constituted by the sight of a man pulling down his trousers in the middle of the street or on a cornerstone? It seems they are only waiting for women to take the same liberties; then they can kill two birds with one stone."[20]

45 - L. M. Bonnet, A beau cacher, (gut verborgen), Kupferstich, 1772
45 - L.M. Bonnet, Well hidden, copperplate engraving, 1772

Doch Merciers Bild von der Weltstadt, „auf der Straße ersonnen, auf dem Randstein geschrieben,"[21] bietet nicht Tatsachen und Sensationen um ihrer selbst willen, sondern dokumentiert den an der Veränderbarkeit und Beseitigung von Mißständen interessierten Blick auf das Chaos der französischen Metropole. Wegen der bereits als modern bezeichneten Reportagetechnik und der willkürlichen Anordnung der einzelnen Stücke kommt die anarchische Vielfalt der riesigen Stadt besonders treffend zum Ausdruck. Mit mehr als 100.000 Exemplaren und mehreren Übersetzungen war Merciers *Tableau* in ganz Europa verbreitet.

Mercier gilt als Ahnherr einer Reihe von Schriftstellern der Großstadt, die von Honoré de Balzac über Eugène Sue und Charles Baudelaire bis zu Leon Paul Fargue und Raymond Quenau reicht. Nun will ich hier nicht von *Zazie dans le métro* 46 und Louis Malles Verfilmung[22] auf Wim Wenders' *Alice in den Städten*[23] kommen und damit zum Film wechseln, vielmehr möchte ich noch ein wenig bei dem in viele einzelne Gemälde aufgelösten Kolossalbild Großstadt/Metropole bleiben, welches die Phantasie oft als „Blick aus dem Fenster" beflügelt hat. 47-48 „‚Da sehen Sie, da ist sie wieder', er deutete auf ein Fenster im zweiten Stock eines vierstöckigen Hauses... ‚Dieses Fenster hat es mir angetan. Da ist immer was los. Mal wird ein Topf herausgesetzt, mal wird an dem Tisch was gemacht, gebügelt, Kuchen geknetet, dann wird der Tisch gedeckt und Blumen darauf gestellt.'"[24]

46 - Umschlag: Raymond Queneau, "Zazie dans le Métro", 1959
46 - Cover: Raymond Queneau, Zazie in the Underground, 1959

47 - Jacob Steinhardt, Die Stadt, 1913
47 - Jacob Steinhardt, The City, 1913

48 - Fernand Léger, Blick aus dem Fenster, 1954
48 - Fernand Léger, View from a window, 1954

Mercier's image of the metropolis "contrived on the street, and written on the curb"[21] does not, however, offer facts and sensations for their own sake, but rather documents a view of the chaos of the French metropolis that is concerned with changing and removing such grievances. The anarchic diversity of the gigantic city is expressed in a particularly striking manner not least because of the reportage technique we have already qualified as modern, but also because of the arbitrary order of the individual pieces. Mercier's *Tableau*, published in more than 100,000 copies and translated into several languages, was read all over Europe.

Mercier could be seen as the forefather of a series of big-city writers, from Honoré de Balzac, to Eugène Sue to Charles Baudelaire, and on to Leon Paul Fargue and Raymond Queneau. At this stage I will abstain from switching to the medium film by way of *Zazie dans le métro* 46 and Louis Malle's film version[22] of the same topic, and from there onto Wim Wenders' *Alice in the Cities*;[23] I would prefer to remain, for a while, with that huge image of the big city/metropolis, broken up into many lesser pictures, which has so often inspired imagination in the form of a "glance out of the window." 47-48 "'Look, there she is again', he was pointing to a window on the second floor of a four storey house. 'I am fascinated by this window. There is always something happening there: a pot being placed outside, working at the table, ironing, kneading dough, then the table is set – flowers are placed on it.'"[24]

49 - Oskar Schlemmer, Wohnraum mit arbeitender Frau, 1942
49 - Oskar Schlemmer, Living room with Working Woman, 1942

50 - Oskar Schlemmer, Am Fenster, 1942
50 - Oskar Schlemmer, At the Window, 1942

51 - Gisèle Freund, Jean Paul Sartre schaut auf St. Germain-des-Près, 1959
51 - Gisèle Freund, Jean Paul Sartre gazes at St. Germain-des-Pres, 1959

52 - Gustave Caillebotte, Homme au balcon, (Mann auf dem Balkon), 1880
52 - Gustave Caillebotte, Man on Balcony, 1880

49-50 Für den Bauhauslehrer Oskar Schlemmer waren seine *Fensterbilder* die künstlerische Umsetzung der Wuppertaler Fenster-Alltagswelten von Gegenüber. Das oder die Zimmer vis-à-vis, die Straßenecke, die Straßenschlucht, 51-52 der Hinterhof, die Hausfassade - nicht nur Voyeure wie Cornell Woolrich oder Edward Hopper spiegeln ihr Stadtbild in dieser Inszenierung. 53-54

53 - Edward Hopper, New Yorker Büro, 1962
53 - Edward Hopper, New York Office, 1962

49-50 For the Bauhaus-teacher Oskar Schlemmer his "window paintings" were a translation of Wuppertal's everyday reality from across the street. That, or the room in relation to the street corner, the gully in the street, 51-52 the back yard, the house façades; not merely voyeurs such as Cornell Woolrich or Edward Hopper have used this type of scenery to reflect their images of the city. 53-54

54 - Edward Hopper, Zimmer in Brooklyn, 1932
54 - Edward Hopper, Room in Brooklyn, 1932

„Es ist Nacht und nach 12 Uhr; ich saß bis zu diesem Augenblick auf einem der beiden kleinen Balkone, die sich vor meinen Fenstern befinden und die mir, da ich in der fünften Etage wohne, eine freie Übersicht über den unendlichen Häuserknäuel der Stadt bis zum Montmartre gestatten; das Zimmer ist wirklich mit seiner Aussicht allerliebst. Über mir der stille Himmel mit schwachem Sterngeflimmer; ein dampfender Schorstein trieb in der Ferne seltsame Rauchwolken in die Höhe; in einer Mansarde, sehr weit von mir, aber doch wegen der offenen Fenster erkennbar, entkleidete sich langsam ein Mädchen, von dem Licht ihres Lämpchens, wie von einer glänzenden Welle umflossen... Die zunächst liegenden Straßen waren dunkel und einsam, besonders diejenige, in die ich unmittelbar hinabsehe, aber die sich weiter oben hinziehenden Boulevards ließen sich an den bis in die obersten Etagen der Häuser hinauf spielenden Lichtreflexen der Laternen noch deutlich unterscheiden,"[25] schreibt bereits 1844 Friedrich Christian Hebbel aus Paris.

Und Marcel Proust assoziiert bei seinem Blick aus dem Fenster eine Aufreihung von Gemälden, ein Bild aus Bildern: „Die außerordentliche Nähe der Häuser im Verhältnis zu den gegenüberliegenden Fenstern, die auf den gleichen Hof gehen, machen aus einem jeden den Rahmen, in dem eine Köchin mit gesenktem Blick vor sich hinträumt, oder in dem etwas weiter fort ein junges Mädchen sich die Haare kämmen läßt von einer Alten ... So bildet jeder Hof für den Nachbarn im nächsten Haus dadurch, daß das Geräusch durch den Zwischenraum unterbunden wird, mit den lautlosen Gesten, die er in einem Rechteck vor Augen führt, welches hinter den geschlossenen Fenstern unter Glas ruht, eine Ausstellung von hundert nebeneinander aufgereihten Bildern holländischer Malerei."[26]

Schon Ende des 19. Jahrhunderts hat kein geringer als Theodor Fontane den Bildcharakter eines großstädtischen Fensterrahmens beschrieben. So als hätte er Proust antipiziert, schildert er den verweilenden Blick auf das zum Gemälde gerinnende Geschehen von gegenüber.

„Jenny..., trat ans Fenster und sah abwechselnd auf den Vorgarten und die Straße. Drüben, im Hause gegenüber, hoch oben in der offenen Mansarde, stand, wie ein Schattenriß in hellem Licht, eine Plätterin, die mit sicherer Hand über das Plättbrett hinfuhr - ja, es war ihr, als höre sie das Mädchen singen. Der Kommerzienrätin Auge mochte von dem anmutigen Bilde nicht lassen..."[27]

"It is night and after twelve; I had been sitting up until now on one of the two small balconies outside my windows that offer me, since I live on the fifth floor, a free view over the endless urban clusters of buildings towards Montmartre; this room really has a great view. Above was the silent sky, lit by the weak twinkling of stars; a puffing chimney sent up strange clouds of smoke in the distance; in a mansard very far off, but recognizable thanks to the open window, a girl was undressing, lit by the light of her lamp, as if enveloped in a glowing wave; the nearby streets were dark and lonely, especially those directly below me, but the boulevards further uptown could still be clearly made out with the light of streetlamps reflecting on the upper storeys of the buildings,"[25] wrote Christian Hebbel as early as 1844 from Paris.
And Marcel Proust associated a series of paintings, a picture of pictures, with his view out of the window:

"The unusual nearness of the buildings in relation to the windows facing one another and giving onto the same courtyard, turn each one into a frame inside which a cook dreams with lowered gaze, or a little further on a young girl has her hair combed by an old woman... In this way each courtyard makes up an exhibition of a hundred Dutch paintings all in a row for the neighbour in the next building, in that sound is hindered by the space between, and he views inside a rectangle the noiseless gestures of whatever happens to be behind the glass of the closed window."[26]

As early as towards the end of the 19th century no one less than Theodor Fontane characterizes the pictorial character of an urban window cut-out. As if anticipating Proust, he describes the lingering glance at an haphazard scene that turns into an instant painting:

"Jenny… stepped up to the window and alternately looked down at the front garden and the street. On the other side, in the house across, high up in the open mansard window, like a silhouette in the bright light an ironing woman stood, who moved a steady hand across the ironing board - yes it seemed to her, as if she would hear the maid sing. The eye of Madam Kommerzienrat would not take leave of this graceful picture…"[27]

55 - George Bellows, Riverfront No. 1 (Coney Island), 1915
55 - George Bellows, Riverfront No. 1 (Coney Island), 1915

Neben der Fülle von Bildeindrücken beschäftigt die Beobachter auch immer wieder die Masse Mensch in ihrer animierenden Vielfalt. 55 „Die Menschen um mich herum hier, boy, ist Babylon - ein melting pot aller Rassen. So stelle ich sie dar. Feine Leute wandeln durch den Central Park - fast vertrocknete liebliche Seidenmumien, bunt, geschminkt - aber auch daneben die zerrissenen Arbeitslosen 56 bums - have a shine Sir - mit ihren niedlichen aufgeräumten Schuhscheinkisten wartend auf den Vorübergehenden, der einen Nickel spenden soll. Viele bunte Neger, reiche und arme, aber alles lustig und meistens sehr kindlich - große Sänger und Tänzer vor dem Herrn ... 57-58 Menschen, 14. Straße, Iren, Italienermamies, dick, mit bambinos, volle - gesteckt volle - Bazare und ein Gewühl von Käufern - alles kleine Leute; billig, unwahrscheinlich billige Preise an Waren, bunt - kein Ende. Manchmal wird man fast schwindlig. Ja, das reizt mich, dieses volle Leben darzustellen,“[28] schreibt George Grosz an Wieland Herzfelde.

56 - George Grosz, Schuhputzer, 1932
56 - George Grosz, Bootblack, 1932

The viewer is not only impressed by the abundance of visual impressions, but also by the masses of people in their stimulating diversity. 55 "The people around me here, boy, it's a Babylon - a melting pot of all races. That's how I'd put it. Elegant people wander through Central Park - charming almost dried out silk mummies, brightly made up - but right next to them are the ragged unemployed 56 bums - have a shine, Sir - with their neat shoe-shine boxes waiting for a passer-by prepared to spend a nickel.
A lot of brightly-coloured Negroes, rich and poor, but on the whole very merry and mostly very childish - big singers and dancers in the eyes of the Lord (...) 57-58
People, 14th Street, Irish, Italian mothers, fat, with bambinos, full - overcrowded - markets and the throng of buyers - all small people, cheap, incredibly cheap prices on the goods, colourful - endless. Sometimes you almost get dizzy. Yes, I find it exciting to depict this full life,"[28] wrote George Grosz to Wieland Herzfelde.

57 - Miguel Covarrubias, Harlem, 1934
57 - Miguel Covarrubias, Harlem, 1934

58 - Mott Street, China Town, New York, 1898
58 - Mott Street, China Town, New York, 1898

Und Theodore Dreiser notiert 1923 ebenfalls in New York: 59-60 „Already at six and six-thirty in the morning they have begun to trickle small streams of human beings Manhattan or cityward, and by seven and seven-fifteen these streams have become sizeable affairs. By seven-thirty and eigth they have changed into heavy, turbulent rivers, and by eight-fifteen and eight-thirty and nine they are raging torrents, no less. They overflow all the streets and avenues and every available means of conveyance. They are pouring into all available doorways, shops, factories, office-buildings - those huge affairs towering so significantly above them."[29]

59 - Umberto Boccioni, Rissa in Galleria, (Aufruhr in der Passage), 1910
59 - Umberto Boccioni, Uproar in the Gallery, 1910

And Theodore Dreiser, also in New York, noted in 1923: 59-60

"Already at six and six-thirty in the morning they have begun to trickle small streams of human beings Manhattan or cityward, and by seven and seven-fifteen these streams have become sizeable affairs. By seven-thirty and eight they have changed into heavy, turbulent rivers, and by eight-fifteen and eight-thirty and nine they are raging torrents, no less. They overflow all the streets and avenues and every available means of conveyance. They are pouring into all available doorways, shops, factories, office-buildings - those huge affairs towering so significantly above them."[29]

60 - Berenice Abbott, Herald Square Manhattan, 16. Juli 1936
60 - Berenice Abbott, Herald Square, Manhattan, July 16, 1936

Die Empfindung, der die Connaisseure und Gourmets der zwanziger Jahre Ausdruck verleihen, hat sich als Stadtbild von Paris und London den Besuchern bereits im 19. 61-62, ja sogar schon im 18. Jahrhundert aufgedrängt:

„In der Mitte der Straße rollt Chaise hinter Chaise, Wagen hinter Wagen und Karren hinter Karren. Durch dieses Getöse, und das Summen und Geräusch von Tausenden von Zungen und Füßen, hören Sie das Geläute von Kirchtürmen, die Glocken der Postbediensteten, die Orgeln, Geigen, Leyern und Tambourinen englischer Savoyarden, und das Heulen derer, die an den Ecken der Gasse unter freiem Himmel kaltes und warmes feil halten. Dann sehen Sie ein Lustfeuer von Hobelspänen Etagen hoch auflodern in einem Kreis von jubilierenden Betteljungen, Matrosen und Spitzbuben,“[30]

so Georg Christoph Lichtenberg 1775 in seinen englischen Briefen über London.
Und noch einmal Christian Friedrich Hebbel über Paris: „In diesem Gewühl von Menschen war gewiß nicht bloß das Geschlecht, die Bildungsstufe und der Stand, sondern jede Spezies bis zur individuellsten herab, repräsentiert, es gab keine bessere Gelegenheit, physiognomische Studien zu machen und die Lücken in meiner Kenntnis des Volks auszustopfen, aber es fehlte an Ruhe; in einer Bibliothek von hunderttausend Bänden kommt man nicht leicht dazu, sich in ein einzelnes Buch zu vertiefen. Ich ließ mich von der großen Welle so mit fortschieben und bückte mich nur hin und wieder nach einer Muschel oder einem bunten Stein.“[31]

The feeling the connoisseurs and gourmets of the nineteen twenties gave expression to had already struck visitors to Paris and London as the image of a city in the nineteenth 61-62 and even the eighteenth centuries:
"Chaise after chaise, carriage after carriage, cart after cart rolls along the middle of the street. Through this din, and the droning and noise of thousands of tongues and feet, you hear the ringing of church bells, the bells of the postal employees, organs, fiddles, lyres and the tambourines of English Savoyards, the shouting of hawkers who sell hot and cold items on the street corners. Then you see a bonfire, several storeys high and made of wood shavings, blaze up inside a circle of jubilant beggar boys, sailors, and rogues"[30] wrote Christoph Lichtenberg in his English letters about London in 1775.

And again Friedrich Christian Hebbel about Paris: "This bustle of people consisted not only of every gender and level of education or class, but also of every human type, down to the most individual; there was no better opportunity to study physiognomy and to fill up the gaps in my knowledge of people, but there was a lack of peace; in a library of a hundred thousand books it is difficult to become absorbed in any single book. So I allowed myself to be carried along by the great wave and only stooped now and again for a mussel or a coloured stone."[31]

61 - Gustave Doré, Durchgangsstraße, 1872
61 - Gustave Doré, A City Throughfare, 1872

62 - Gustave Doré, Ludgate Hill, 1872
62 - Gustave Doré, Ludgate Hill, 1872

Es quirlt, überflutet, brandet, schwillt an, ebbt ab gleich den Gezeiten. „A city is like a great hungry sea, which flows on and on, filling up every creek and overspreads its borders, flooding the plains beyond,“[32] kommentiert Arthur Sherwell in seinem *Life in West London* 1901. Die Metapher vom Ozean, 63 vom steinernen Meer, von der Stadt, die das Land überflutet und in immer wieder neuen Wellenringen der Peripherie eine neue Peripherie vorlagert, umfaßt auch die Wahrnehmung der vielschichtigen kakophonischen, aber auch symphonischen Geräusche in der Metropole.

Symphonie Berlin betitelt Fritz Engel 1931 ein Gedicht:

„Riesenorchester, aufschwärmend in Tönen,
Ein Brausen, ein Rauschen, ein Rollen, ein Dröhnen,
Des Lebens Gesänge, der Arbeit Gesänge,
Ein Sichverketten, ein Lösen der Klänge,
Grelles und Schnelles - der Wagen Geklirre,
Der Drohruf der Hupen, der Menschen Geschwirre,
Ein wanderndes, wogendes, wälzendes Heer -
Und immer mehr...“[33]

It swirls, floods, surges, swells and ebbs just like the tide. "A city is like a great hungry sea, which flows on and on, filling up every creek and overspreads its borders, flooding the plains beyond,"[32] comments Arthur Sherwell in his *Life in West London*, 1901. The metaphor of the sea, 63 of the stone sea, of the city that floods the countryside and lays periphery beyond periphery in ever-expanding ripples also embraces the perception of the many-layered cacophonic but also symphonic sound associated with the metropolis:

Symphonie Berlin is the title of Fritz Engel's 1931 poem:

"Gigantic orchestra,
with surging tones,
A roaring, rushing, rolling, droning,
Of life's hymn, work's hymn,
An interlinking, a release of sounds,
Sharp and quick - the clatter of cars,
The warning call of horns, the bustle of people,
A wandering, swaying, rolling army,
And more and more..."[33]

63 - Werner Heldt, Berlin am Meer, 1952
63 - Werner Heldt, Berlin-on-Sea, 1952

Diese Orchestrierung erhält theatralische und szenographische Unterstützung durch die Berücksichtigung von Tag, Nacht und Wetter. Die „Ohnehin-Schon-Dramatik“ wird, getaucht in Sonnen-, und Sonnenuntergangslicht 64 oder die Kunstlichter der Nacht widerspiegelnd noch gesteigert. „Es dämmerte, wie wir den Père-Lachaise verließen und es war ganz dunkel, als wir die Boulevards St-Martin wieder erreichten; durch eine Straße hindurch sahen wir auf den Montmartre, 65 der in einer wahrhaft phantastischen Beleuchtung vor uns lag, man glaubte nichts Wirkliches, Wahrhaftes zu sehen, sondern eine Kulisse aus einer Wunder-Oper.“[34] Was noch bei Hebbel städtische Vedoute und literarisches Genrebild ist, wird als Beleuchtung der elektrifizierten Metropole 66-67 und als zuckende Lichtbänder später zu einem eigenständigen Thema der Literatur, der Malerei, der Fotocollage und des Films. Dabei wird die Heldin Großstadt abwechselnd in Kunstlicht, Naturlicht und die jeweiligen Wettereffekte getaucht. Robert Musil und Alfred Döblin stülpen eine Wetternachricht über ihre Montagen aus Momentaufnahmen, Nachrichten und Handlung.

64 - Craig McPherson, Herbst, 1980
64 - Craig McPherson, Autumn, 1980

65 - Montmartre, Sonnenuntergang, 1990
65 - Montmartre, Sunset, 1990

66 - Lichtreklame Bond Clothing Store, New York City, 1948-54
66 - Neon advertisement, Bond Clothing Store, New York, 1948-54

67 - Nächtlich beleuchteter Dachgarten des Hotels Astor am Broadway, New York City, um 1908
67 - Illuminated roof garden at night, Hotel Astor on Broadway, New York, 1908

This orchestration can count on a very special theatrical or scenic effect depending on whether it takes place by day or at night, and during different weather conditions. The "dramatic per se" is enhanced when bathed in the rays of the sun, 64 or the sunset, or when it reflects the artificial light of night. "It was twilight as we left Père-Lachaise and it was quite dark when we got to the Boulevard St-Martin; we could see up a street to Montmartre 65 that lay before us in a truly fantastic light; it was hard to believe that what we saw was real and not the scenery of some wondrous opera."[34] What is no more than an urban veduta and a typical literary image in the work of Hebbel, later becomes the illumination of the electrified metropolis, 66-67 the flickering strips of light a self-sufficient theme of literature, painting, photo-collage and film. The heroine, the great city herself, is shown partly in an artificial light, partly in a natural light and in different weather conditions. A weather report becomes a set of conditioning brackets that Robert Musil and Alfred Döblin clamp around their montages assembled out of snapshots, news items and actions.

Musil eröffnet seinen Roman *Der Mann ohne Eigenschaften* folgendermaßen: „Über dem Atlantik befand sich ein barometrisches Minimum; es wanderte ostwärts, einem über Rußland lagernden Maximum zu, und verriet noch nicht die Neigung, diesem nördlich auszuweichen. Die Isothermen und Isotheren taten ihre Schuldigkeit. ... Mit einem Wort, das das Tatsächliche recht gut bezeichnet, wenn es auch etwas altmodisch ist: Es war ein schöner Augusttag des Jahres 1913,“[35] als seine Heldin die Großstadt und ihre Protagonisten die Bühne betreten: „Autos schossen aus schmalen Straßen in die Seichtigkeit heller Plätze. 68 Fußgängerdunkelheit bildete wolkige Schnüre. Wo kräftigere Striche der Geschwindigkeit quer durch ihre lockere Eile fuhren, verdickten sie sich, rieselten nachher rascher und hatten nach wenigen Schwingungen wieder ihren gleichmäßigen Puls. Hunderte Töne waren zu einem drahtigen Geräusch ineinander verwunden, aus dem einzelne Spitzen vorstanden, längs dessen schneidige Kanten liefen und sich wieder einebneten, von dem klare Töne absplitterten und verflogen ... Städte lassen sich an ihrem Gang erkennen wie Menschen ... Es soll also auf den Namen der Stadt kein besonderer Wert gelegt werden. Wie alle großen Städte bestand sie aus Unregelmäßigkeit, Wechsel, Vorgleiten, Nichtschritthalten, Zusammenstößen von Dingen und Angelegenheiten, bodenlosen Punkten der Stille dazwischen aus Bahnen und Ungebahntem, aus einem großen rhythmischen Schlag und der ewigen Verstimmung und Verschiebung aller Rhythmen gegeneinander, und gleich im ganzen einer kochenden Blase, die in einem Gefäß ruht, das aus dem dauerhaften Stoff von Häusern, Gesetzen, Verordnungen und geschichtlichen Überlieferungen besteht.“[36]

68 - Cor van Eesteren, Straßenkreuzung in Paris, um 1925
68 - Cor van Eesteren, Street intersection in Paris, ca. 1925

Musil begins his novel *The Man without Qualities* as follows: "There was a depression over the Atlantic. It was travelling eastwards, towards an area of high pressure over Russia, and still showed no tendency to move northwards around it. The isotherms and isotheres were fulfilling their functions." [...] "In short, to use an expression that describes the facts pretty satisfactorily, even though it is somewhat old-fashioned: it was a fine August day in the year 1913,"[35] when his heroine the metropolis and her various protagonists come on the scene:

"Motor cars came shooting out of deep, narrow streets into the shallow of bright squares. 68 Dark patches of pedestrian bustle formed into cloudy streams. Where stronger lines of speed transected their loose-woven hurrying, they clotted up only to trickle on all the faster then and after a few ripples regain their regular pulse-beat. Hundreds of sounds were intertwined into a coil of wiry noise, with single barbs projecting, sharp edges running along it and submerging again, and clear notes splintering off flying and scattering. (...)

Cities can be recognized by their pace just as people can by their walk. (...) So no special significance should be attached to the name of the city. Like all big cities, it consisted of irregularity, change, sliding forward, not keeping in step, collisions of things and affairs, and fathomless points of silence in between, of paved ways and wilderness, of one great rhythmic throb and the perpetual discord and dislocation of all opposing rhythms, and as a whole resembled a seething, bubbling fluid in a vessel consisting of the solid material of buildings, laws, regulations, and historical traditions."[36]

Ähnlich geht Alfred Döblin in seinem Roman *Berlin Alexanderplatz*[37] vor. Der Platz erscheint als eigenständiges, komplexes Lebewesen, vor allem durch die reflexive Form: das strömt in sich, geht von sich aus und lenkt die Bewegungen wieder auf sich zurück. Genauso erfaßt denn auch die folgende Beschreibung den Platz als Raum. 69 Ein von Passanten und Fahrzeugen dicht belebter Kreis, der strahlenförmig Straßen in den weiteren Umkreis der Stadt entläßt, der Menschen ausströmt und einsaugt nach und von allen Richtungen - Startpunkt und Umschlagort in einem. Folgerichtig setzt der Erzähler seinen Weg fort in den konkreten Berliner Alltag hinein. Indem er vorab den Wetterbericht mitteilt, bewirkt er ein Doppeltes. Einmal beschreibt er mit wissenschaftlichem Gestus die atmosphärische Hülle, die an diesem Tag alle Bewohner Berlins betrifft. Zudem holt er den Leser eng an den Gegenstand heran, indem er ihn den Wortlaut der meteorologischen Meldung teilen läßt mit denjenigen, die den Rosenthaler Platz und das übrige Berlin bevölkern. Dann greift er zu einem Mittel, das, wiederum aufs vereinzelte, im Ganzen der Stadt verwahrte Konkrete zielend, im Verlauf des Romans immer wieder gute Dienste leisten wird. Er nimmt eine bestimmte Trambahn – hier die 68, die gerade den Platz kreuzt - zum Anlaß, um sämtliche wichtigen Haltestellen auf ihrer Strecke aufzuzählen: Wittenau, Nordbahnhof, Heilanstalt, Weddingplatz, Stettiner Bahnhof usw. Ob der Leser diese Haltestellen durch Ortskenntnis verifizieren kann oder nicht - ihre Namen rufen, da sie mit der Straßenbahnlinie eine Linie durch die Stadt ziehen, deren topographische Fülle auf.[38]

Fülle und Masse werden in montierten Assoziationsketten bewältigt. Döblin benutzt die Montage auch als produktionstechnisches Prinzip, indem er Zeitungsausschnitte ohne jeglichen Bruch in seinen Romantext aufnimmt, wie das übrigens Thomas Mann mit lexikalischen Quellen im *Zauberberg*[39] handhabt und Uwe Johnson in den *Jahrestagen*[40] mit der Berichterstattung aus der *New York Times*.

69 - Richard Matz, Weltstadtverkehr Berlin, Alexanderplatz, um 1933
69 - Richard Matz, Metropolitan City Traffic in Berlin, Alexanderplatz, ca. 1933

Alfred Döblin uses a similar approach in his novel *Berlin Alexanderplatz*.[37] The square appears as a self-sufficient and complex life-form. First reflexively: it flows within itself, sends currents out and then brings the motion back into itself again. The following description of the square as a space follows the same tenor. 69 A circle, densely populated by pedestrians and vehicles, sends radial streets out into the wide circumference of the city. People are sent out in all directions and sucked back in from all directions - a starting point and transit station in one. As is to be expected, the narrator continues his way into the actual everyday life of Berlin. The fact that he gives us the weather report in advance has a double effect. On the one hand he indicates in a scientific manner the atmospheric envelope that affects all Berlin inhabitants on that day. Furthermore, he brings his readers into close contact with the objective situation in that he allows them to share the meteorological report with those living in Rosenthaler Platz and the rest of Berlin.

He then resorts to a method which will serve him repeatedly throughout the novel, again aimed at the undifferentiated and concrete elements present in the whole city. He takes a random tram line - here the number 68 - which happens to be crossing the square at that moment -; he then enumerates some of the important stops on its route: Wittenau, Nordbahnhof, Heilanstalt, Weddingplatz, Stettiner Bahnhof, etc. Whether or not the readers can verify these stops through their knowledge of the city, the names conjure up its topographical diversity, since they draw the city together along a dotted line tracing the tram route.[38]

Abundance and the masses are dealt with in montages of chains of association. Döblin also uses the montage as a principle of technical production by randomly inserting newspaper cuttings into the text of his novel, a technique also employed by Thomas Mann, who inserts lexical sources in his *The Magic Mountain*,[39] or Uwe Johnson in *Jahrestage*[40] with reports from the *New York Times*.

Mit der Montage[41] versucht die Kunst, die von den veränderten Produktionsweisen bestimmte industrielle Welt mit deren eigenen Mitteln in die Schranken zu weisen,
70 indem sie das Fremde in der Entfremdung durch Montage des Heterogenen gleichsam einem neuen Kontext unterordnet. Damit verlangt sie jedoch gleichzeitig vom Rezipienten die Bereitschaft und Anstrengung für eine neue Lesart. Angestrebt ist ein Effekt des Diskontinuierlichen; eine Sinngebung, die Materialien, die nicht zusammenpassen, aus ihren Herkunfts- und Funktionszusammenhängen reißt, um sie in der künstlerischen Behandlung zu einer neuen Entität zusammenzufügen, die dann wiederum geeignet ist, gerade auch über den ursprünglichen Zusammenhang eine Aussage zu machen. Die Montagetechnik findet selbstverständlich nicht nur in den bereits genannten Romanen oder in James Joyce's *Ulysses*[42] oder John Dos Passos' *Manhattan Transfer*[43] als Dokumenten einer „Zeit-Montage" ihren Ausdruck, sondern ist u.a. Teil vieler Fotobücher und Theaterinszenierungen der Zwanziger Jahre.

70 - Paul Citroën, Metropolis, 1923
70 - Paul Citroën, Metropolis, 1923

71 - El Lissitzky, Die Läufer, 1930
71 - El Lissitzky, The runners, 1930

Art attempts to consign the industrial world, with its altered processes of production, back into place by employing its own methods. 70 The alien, through alienation by means of a montage[41] of heterodox elements, is thus placed in a new context. At the same time art requires of anyone approaching it a readiness and the effort required for a new way of reading. The aim here is an effect of discontinuity, a granting of meaning which removes incompatible materials from their original and functional relationships in order to unite them in a new entity by means of an artistic treatment, which is then in a position to make statements about the original context. Montage techniques are not, of course, only found in the above-mentioned novels, in James Joyce's *Ulysses*[42] or John Dos Passos' *Manhattan Transfer*;[43] they are also evident in many photographic books and theatre stage designs of the twenties.

72 - El Lissitzky, Der Läufer, 1930
72 - El Lissitzky, The runner, 1930

Neben den Collagen der Dadaisten oder den Fotocollagen von El Lissitzky 71-72 verweise ich hier auf die Zusammenarbeit von László Moholy-Nagy und Walter Mehring in *Der Kaufmann von Berlin*[44] oder John Heartfields satirisch-kritische Arbeit für Kurt Tucholskys *Deutschland, Deutschland über alles*.[45] 73-74

73 - László Moholy-Nagy, Projektionsfotomontage für ein Bühnenbild zu Walter Mehrings „Der Kaufmann von Berlin“, 1929
73 - László Moholy-Nagy, Photomontage as projection for a stage setting for Walter Mehring's "The Merchant of Berlin", 1929

I am referring here not only to the collages of the Dadaists and El Lissitzky's photocollages, 71-72 but also to László Moholy-Nagy's and Walter Mehring's joint work on *Der Kaufmann von Berlin*[44] and Heartfield's satirical-critical work for Kurt Tucholsky's *Deutschland, Deutschland über alles*.[45] 73-74

74 - John Heartfield, Schutzumschlag für Kurt Tucholsky: „Deutschland, Deutschland über alles", 1929
74 - John Heartfield, Dust cover for Kurt Tucholsky's "Germany, Germany Above All", 1929

75 - Fotomontage für den Film „Berlin. Die Sinfonie der Großstadt", 1927
75 - Photomontage for the film: "Berlin, The Symphony of the Big City", 1927

Nicht nur ein Klassiker der Filmkunst, sondern ein Musterbeispiel für einen Montagefilm ist Walter Ruttmanns *Berlin. Die Sinfonie der Großstadt*[46] (1927). 75-76 Der Film war als außergewöhnlicher Versuch, das Wesen der Metropole zu fassen, so populär, daß ihm eine Reihe Imitationen folgten: *Symphonie urbaine*, Mexiko 1929, und *Symphonie d'une métropole*, Tokyo 1929. Das verschiedentlich in diesem Zusammenhang zitierte New York-Porträt *42nd Street*[47] 77 hält einem Vergleich nicht stand. Es ist ein reiner Revue-Film. Montiert sind hier lediglich die Wolkenkratzer-Architekturen auf die zu Figurinen stilisierten Balettänzer, die sich als Gebäudekörper auf den Treppenstufen hin und her wiegen.

76 - Fotomontage für „Berlin. Die Sinfonie der Großstadt", 1927
76 - Photomontage for the film: "Berlin, The Symphony of the Big City", 1927

Walter Ruttmann's *Berlin. Die Sinfonie der Großstadt*[46] (1927) 75-76 is not only a classic of cinema, but also an exemplary montage film. This unusual attempt at capturing the essence of the metropolis on film was so popular that it inspired a series of imitations: *Symphonie urbaine*, Mexico 1929 and *Symphonie d'une métropole*, Tokyo 1929 are only two examples. *42nd Street*,[47] 77 the Portrait of New York, so often referred to in this context, does not bear comparison. It is a revue film. The only montage element here is the skyscraper architecture that alternates with the ballet dancers, stylized as building-like figurines that sway to and fro on the steps of the stage.

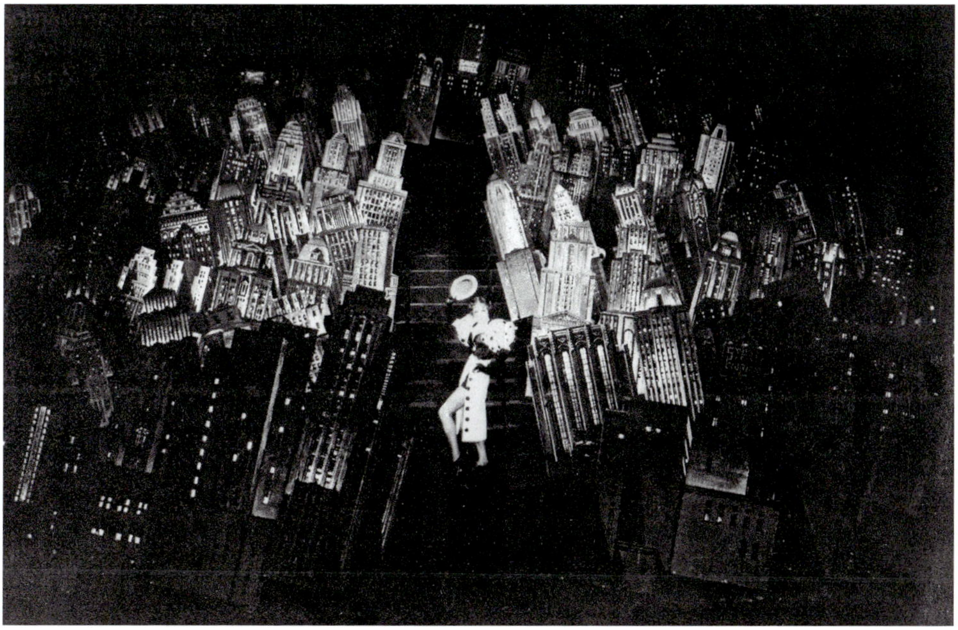

77 - Lloyd Bacon, „42nd Street", Standbild, 1933
77 - Lloyd Bacon, "42nd Street", film still, 1933

Ruttmanns Film ist nicht nur wegen seiner Montagetechnik bemerkenswert. In seinem Porträt zitiert er über einen Zeitraum von vierundzwanzig Stunden auch die unterschiedlichsten sozialen Schichten auf die Bühne. 78-79 Die Arbeitslosen, die Arbeiter, die Angestellten, die Müßiggänger, die Bankdirektoren und die Aufsichtsratsvorsitzenden versinnbildlichen gleichzeitig auch die Schatten- und die Sonnenseiten der Metropole, und wie das Phänomen der Masse fordern sie die Phantasie der Maler, Dichter, Fotografen und Regisseure heraus.

78 - Walter Ruttmann, „Berlin. Die Sinfonie der Großstadt", Standbild, 1927
78 - Walter Ruttmann, "Berlin, The Symphony of the Big City", film still, 1927

Ruttmann's film is remarkable not only for its montage technique. In only twenty-four hours he managed to drag a number of different social classes onto the stage. 78-79 Unemployed, workers, idlers, bank directors and chairmen of boards together symbolize the shadowy and sunny sides of the metropolis and fire the imagination of painters, poets, photographers and filmmakers just as much as the phenomenon of the masses.

79 - Walter Ruttmann, „Berlin. Die Sinfonie der Großstadt", Standbild, 1927
79 - Walter Ruttmann, "Berlin, The Symphony of the Big City", film still, 1927

Die Stadt als Bedrohung

Volker Klotz benennt in seinem Buch *Die erzählte Stadt* ein Kapitel: „Agon Stadt"[48] und verweist damit darauf, „daß das Stadtleben den Kampf für den Nahrungserwerb mit der Natur in einen Kampf um den Menschen verwandelt hat, daß der umkämpfte Gewinn hier nicht von der Natur, sondern von Menschen gewährt wird."[49]

„Build your cities proud and high. Lay your sewers. Span your rivers. Work feverishly. Sleep dreamlessly. Sing madly, like the bulbul. Underneath below the deepest foundations, there lives another race of men. They are dark, somber, passionate. They muscle into the bowels of the earth. They wait with a patience which is terrifying. They are the scavengers, the devourers, the avengers. They emerge when everything topples into dust."[50] 80

Dieses apokalyptische Bild, welches Henry Miller hier in *Sexus* heraufbeschwört, ließe sich ohne weiteres als Kurzbeschreibung von Fritz Langs Film *Metropolis*[51] verwenden. 81

80 - Erich Kettelhut, Zeichnung für Fritz Langs „Metropolis", 1927
80 - Erich Kettelhut, drawing for Fritz Lang's film "Metropolis", 1927

The City as a Threat

Volker Klotz called one chapter in his book *Die erzählte Stadt*[48] (The Narrated City) *Agon Stadt* (Agon City), referring to the fact "that the city has turned the struggle with nature for food into a struggle of human beings with themselves, that the profit people are fighting for here is not yielded by nature, but by people."[49]

"Build your cities proud and high. Lay your sewers. Span your rivers. Work feverishly. Sleep dreamlessly. Sing madly, like the bulbul. Underneath, below the deepest foundations, there lives another race of men. They are dark, sombre, passionate. They muscle into the bowels of the earth. They wait with a patience which is terrifying. They are the scavengers, the devourers, the avengers. They emerge when everything topples into dust."[50] 80
The apocalyptic picture Henry Miller conjures up here in *Sexus* could easily be used as a summary of Fritz Lang's film *Metropolis*.[51] 81

81 - Filmplakat „Metropolis", 1927
81 - Film Poster for "Metropolis", 1927

„... bei der Besichtigung New Yorks hatte ich die Vorstellung, daß dies der Schmelztiegel vielfältiger und wirrer menschlicher Kräfte war, die blind einander anstießen, in dem unbezwingbaren Verlangen sich gegenseitig auszubeuten, und so in einer ständigen Angst lebten. Den ganzen Tag bin ich in den Straßen herumgelaufen. Die Gebäude erschienen mir wie ein vertikaler Vorhang, schimmernd und sehr leicht, ein üppiger Bühnenhintergrund, an einem düsteren Himmel aufgehängt, um zu blenden, zu zerstreuen und zu hypnotisieren. Nachts vermittelte die Stadt ausschließlich den Eindruck zu leben: sie lebte wie Illusionen leben. Ich wußte, daß ich über all diese Eindrücke einen Film machen mußte,"[52] schreibt Lang 1924 aus New York. Fritz Lang war am 3. Oktober 1924 in Hamburg an Bord des Passagierschiffes „Deutschland" gegangen. Langs Eindrükke von der Stadt wie auch die des ersten Anblicks der Stadtsilhouette, wie er sie später im *Film-Kurier* publizierte, ähneln denen Erich Mendelsohns. Beide waren an Bord desselben Schiffes und dies in angeregtem Kontakt miteinander. Hier Mendelsohns Eindruck am 11. Oktober 1924 vom Deck der „Deutschland" aus: „Gegen Mittag Land in Sicht... Plötzlich aus Abendnebeln für einen Augenblick - Woolworth Building. Schemenhaft, hoch oben im Himmel. Niemand dachte so hoch hinauf... Lichter knapp über der Meerbucht, ansteigend, aufgereckt in den Himmel - rotes Licht - Woolworthspitze. Das Schiff macht einen Bogen - Babylon - Geisterhaft im Monddunkel. Hochgerissen mit Lichtvertikalen. Schnelle Einfahrt, Wendungen, Kurven - Raumschlacht im Dunkel, im Licht der eingebetteten Straßen. Stoß ins Herz, verloren in solchem Ausmaß - Tragik des Wahnsinns, wahnsinnige Macht, Raummacht, unendlicher Siegesrausch."[53] Ähnlich wie in Henry Millers Schilderung könnte sich dies als Antizipation zu *Metropolis* lesen lassen. *Metropolis*, dessen Handlung nicht der Melodramatik entbehrt, ist vor allem wegen seiner Filmarchitektur 82-83 und seiner „special effects" berühmt geworden.

82 - Erich Kettelhut, Stadtansicht für den Film „Metropolis", 1927
82 - Erich Kettelhut, view of the city for the film "Metropolis", 1927

83 - Filmarchitektur für den Film „Metropolis", 1927
83 - Film architecture for the film "Metropolis", 1927

"...when visiting New York, I imagined that this was the melting pot of a variety and confusion of human energies that blindly clashed together in an unquenchable urge for mutual exploitation, and therefore lived in constant fear. I wandered around the streets all day. The buildings seemed like a vertical curtain, shimmering and very light, a luxurious stage set, hung up on a dark sky in order to dazzle, to distract and to hypnotize. Only at night the city gave the impression of being alive: it lived as an illusion lives. I knew that I would have to make a film about all of these impressions,"[52] wrote Lang from New York in 1924. On October 3rd Fritz Lang went on board the ocean liner "Deutschland" in Hamburg. Lang's impressions of the city as well as the first glimpse of the skyline, described by him later in *Film-Kurier*, resemble those of Erich Mendelsohn. Both - in a vivid contact with each other - were on board the same liner. Mendelsohn's characterization is the following: "noon land in sight... Suddenly, appearing for a moment out of the evening mist - the Woolworth Building. Just the outlines, towering up in the sky. No one ever thought that high... Lights just above the bay, ascending, stretching up into the sky - red light - the top of Woolworth. The ship turns - Babylon - ghostly in the moonlit darkness. Towering up with verticals of light. Rapid entry, turns, curves - a battle of spaces in the darkness, in the light of the embedded streets. A thrust to the heart, lost in such dimensions - the tragedy of madness, insane power, the power of space, the unending intoxication of victory."[53] Similar to Henry Miller's description, thiscould be read as an anticipation of *Metropolis*. Though the film does not lack melodramatic elements, *Metropolis* is still known above all for its film architecture 82-83 and special effects.

Er ebnete den Weg zu einer ganzen Reihe von Science-fiction-Stadt-Filmen 84-85 wie *High Treason* (1929) oder *Just Imagine* (1930) bis hin zu *Blade Runner* (1982).[54] 86-87

84 - David Butler, „Just Imagine", Standbild, 1930
84 - David Butler, "Just Imagine", film still, 1930

85 - David Butler, „Just Imagine", Standbild, 1930
85 - David Butler, "Just Imagine", film still, 1930

It paved the way for a whole series of urban science-fiction films 84-85 from *High Treason* (1929) or *Just Imagine* (1930) to *Blade Runner* (1982).[54] 86-87

86 - Ridley Scott, „Blade Runner", Standbild, 1982
86 - Ridley Scott, "Blade Runner", film still, 1982

87 - Ridley Scott, „Blade Runner", Standbild, 1982
87 - Ridley Scott, "Blade Runner", film still, 1982

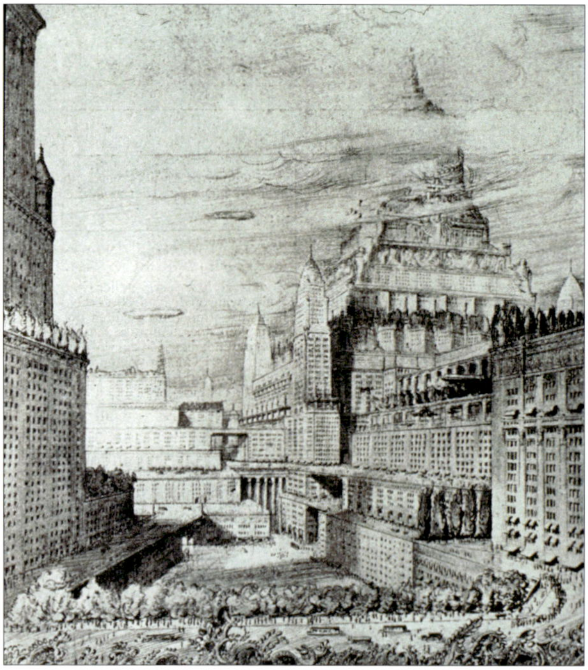

88 - Illustration aus: „King's Views of New York", 1911/12
88 - Illustration from "King's Views of New York", 1911/12

89 - Titelseite aus: „King's Views of New York", 1911/12
89 - Cover of "King's Views of New York", 1911/12

Ob Moses Kings *Views of New York* von 1911/12 88-89 oder Hugh Ferriss' Visionen ab 1922 für *Metropolis* Pate gestanden haben,[55] 90-91 möchte ich nicht weiter analysieren. Hier geht es im folgenden um das immer wieder zitierte Bild von der guten und der bösen Stadt.

90 - Hugh Ferriss, Die Stadt bei Nacht, Abstieg in die Straßen, 1925
90 - Hugh Ferriss, The City at Night, Descent into the Streets, 1925

91 - Hugh Ferriss, Hochhausgedränge, 1926
91 - Hugh Ferriss, Crowding Towers, 1926

I do not want to enter into the discussion about whether Moses King's *Views of New York*, made in 1911/12, 88-89 or Hugh Ferriss' visions from 1922 on 90-91 could be seen as possible influences here.[55] I would rather like to focus on the repeatedly cited image of a good and an evil city.

92 - Porträt von Charles Dickens mit Szenen seiner Romane
92 - Portrait of Charles Dickens with scenes from his novels

Bei den Kritikern der Großstadt wird die Metropole zu einem Sündenbabel, von einer Verrohung der Sitten, ja vom Untergang der Kultur ist die Rede. Von Louis-Sébastien Merciers *Tableau de Paris* über Eugène Sues' *Les Mysteres de Paris*,[56] der Behandlung der „dark sides" bei Charles Dickens 92-93 bis zu den Skizzen und Fotografien von Heinrich Zille 94-95 und Käthe Kollwitz 96-97 oder den bissigen Dokumenten von George Grosz werden die Schattenseiten großstädtischer Lebensbedingungen aufgedeckt.

93 - Illustration zur Theateraufführung „Oliver Twist“, London, 1905
93 - Illustration for the theatre performance of "Oliver Twist", London, 1905

Critics of large cities see the metropolis as a Babel of sin and speak of a brutalization of morals and even the decline of culture. The shadow sides of metropolitan life were uncovered by a whole line of individuals, from Louis-Sébastien Mercier's *Tableau de Paris*, to Eugène Sues' *Les Mystères de Paris*,[56] from the "dark sides" of Charles Dickens 92-93 to sketches and photographs by Heinrich Zille 94-95 and Käthe Kollwitz 96-97 or George Grosz's biting documents.

94 - Waldemar Titzenthaler, Berlin, Am Krögel, 1897
94 - Waldemar Titzenthaler, Berlin, Am Krögel, 1897

95 - Heinrich Zille, Frau und Kinder auf der Knobelsdorffbrücke in Charlottenburg, 1900
95 - Heinrich Zille, Woman and Children on Knobelsdorff Bridge in Berlin-Charlottenburg, 1900

Armut und Kriminalität werden oft von den Verbesserungen anstrebenden - also nicht kulturpessimistischen - Kritikern als Ursache und Folge behandelt. Sichtweisen, wie sie - selbstverständlich vor einem anderen Hintergrund - Charlie Chaplin als Parodie unter anderem in seinen Filmen *The Kid* (1919/1920) 98 und *City Lights* (1930/1931) oder davor der New Yorker Fotograf Jacob A. Riis in seinem 1890 veröffentlichten Buch *How the Other Half Lives*[57] dokumentiert haben. 99-100

96 - Käthe Kollwitz, Weihnacht, 1910
96 - Käthe Kollwitz, Christmas, 1910

97 - Käthe Kollwitz, Ins Wasser, 1909
97 - Käthe Kollwitz, Into the Water, 1909

98 - Charlie Chaplin, „The Kid", Standbild, 1921
98 - Charlie Chaplin, "The Kid", film still, 1921

Poverty and crime are often treated as cause and consequence by critics striving for improvement, in other words not the culturally pessimistic critics. Views that have been documented, though obviously against a different background, by Charlie Chaplin in the form of parody in his films *The Kid* (1919/1920) 98 and *City Lights* (1930/1931), or even before that by the New York photographer Jacob A. Riis in his book *How the Other Half Lives*,[57] published in 1929. 99-100

99 - Jacob A. Rijs, Lebten nirgendwo, 1890
99 - Jacob A. Rijs, Didn´t Live Nowhere, 1890

100 - Jacob A. Riis, Griechische Kinder in Gotham Court, 1890
100 - Jacob A. Rijs, Greek children in Gotham Court, 1890

Selbst Friedrich Schiller plante 1799, beeinflußt durch Merciers *Tableau* das Porträt der Metropole Paris in einem Drama mit dem Titel *Die Polizei*. Die auf der Projektion einer Bedrohung basierende Großstadtfeindschaft wird im deutschsprachigen Raum um 1900 bei vielen konservativen Bildungsbürgern zu einem quasi-religiösen Bekenntnis. Vereinfacht ausgedrückt, speist sich diese Feindschaft aus der platten Gegenüberstellung von Stadt = Böse und Land = Gut.

In Frankreich wiederum findet Victor Hugo die folgende Formulierung für den hier angesprochenen Gegensatz: „Die Städte mit ihrer Verderbnis lassen die Menschen verrohen. Die Berge, das Meer und der Wald lassen sie zwar verwildern; sie fördern ihre rauhen Seiten, doch ohne ihre menschlichen durchweg zu zerstören."[58]

Ein wenig bekannter, aber dennoch durchaus beachtenswerter Film Luis Trenkers verdeutlicht auf sehr plakative Weise diesen doch eher komplexen Gegensatz. Trenker kontrastiert in einem filmischen Schwarz-Weiß-Gemälde die kalte, böse, inhumane Stadt mit der Wärme und Geborgenheit des Lebens auf dem Lande. *Der verlorene Sohn*[59] von 1934 ist eines der seltenen filmischen Dokumente, die die Auswirkungen der Depression als Verelendung vieler Menschen in New York zeigen 101-102 - allerdings zur Idealisierung von Heimat und Scholle.

101 - Berenice Abbott, Talman Street, Brooklyn, 1936
101 - Berenice Abbott, Talman Street, Brooklyn, 1936

Even Friedrich Schiller planned a portrait of Paris in 1799, influenced by Mercier's *Tableau*, in the form of a drama entitled *Die Polizei* (The Police). In the German speaking world a dislike of the metropolis, based on its identification with the concept of threat, became almost a religious doctrine among many educated conservatives around 1900. In simple terms, this enmity was inspired by the crude opposition of city = bad and country = good.

In France Victor Hugo characterizes this oppositon as follows: "Cities in their balefulness make people coarse. Mountains, the sea and the wood make them running to seed, they further people's raw attitudes without destroying their humaneness."[58]

A little known, but nonetheless admirable film by Luis Trenker makes this rather complex opposition plain in a very striking fashion. Trenker contrasts the cold, evil, inhumane city with the warmth and safety of life in the country in a cinematic black and white painting. *Der verlorene Sohn*,[59] 1934, is one of the few film documents to show the effects of the Depression in the destitution of a great number of people in New York, 101-102 although admittedly in an idealization of the mother country and her soil.

102 - Jacob A. Riis, New York. Auf dem Dach der Baracken, 1890
102 - Jacob A. Rijs, New York. On the Roof of the shanties, 1890

Ihre Nahrung findet diese Dämonisierung der Großstadt u.a. bei Friedrich Nietzsche, in dessen *Zarathustra* es heißt: „Wehe dieser großen Stadt - und ich wollte ich sähe die Feuersäule, in der sie verbrannt wird!“[60] 103-104

„Denn Herr die grossen Städte sind verlorene und aufgelöste, wie Flucht vor Flammen ist die größte, - und ist kein Trost, daß er sie tröste, und ihre kleine Zeit vernimmt. Da leben Menschen, leben schlecht und schwer, ...“[61]

schreibt Rainer Maria Rilke 1903.

Auch in Oswald Spenglers zwischen 1918 und 1922 erschienenem vielbeachteten und umstrittenen kulturphilosophischen Werk *Der Untergang des Abendlandes. Umrisse zu einer Morphologie der Weltgeschichte*[62] werden Entartung und Verfall als Phänomene der Dekadenz der Großstadt, der Weltstadt angelastet. „Der Steinkoloß Weltstadt steht am Ende des Lebenslaufes einer jeden großen Kultur.“[63] Aber er muß gleichzeitig auch konstatieren: „Wer einmal der ganzen sündhaften Schönheit dieses letzten Wunders aller Geschichte verfallen ist, der befreit sich nicht wieder... das Heimweh nach der großen Stadt ist stärker vielleicht als jedes andere.“[64]

103 - Martha Diamond, Downtown, 1981
103 - Martha Diamond, Downtown, 1981

This demonising of the city can be traced back - amongst others - to Friedrich Nietzsche, who wrote in *Zarathustra*: "Woe unto this great city, and I wish I could see the column of fire in which it will be consumed!"[60] 103-104

"For the great cities, Oh Lord, are lost and stray, the greatest is no more than the flight from flames, - and it is no comfort that He should comfort them and watch over their short time. People live there, and live hard and badly..."[61] wrote Rainer Maria Rilke in 1903.
In Oswald Spengler's popular and controversial work *Der Untergang des Abendlandes. Umrisse einer Morphologie der Weltgeschichte* (The Decline of the West. Outline for a Morphology of World History),[62] written between 1918 and 1922, degeneration and decay are also alleged as phenomena in the decadence of the big city, the metropolis. "The stone colossus of a metropolis stands at the end of the life of every great culture."[63] But he has to concede at the same time that "Anyone who has ever fallen for the whole sinful beauty of this last wonder of history can never again free himself ... homesickness for a big city is perhaps stronger than any other."[64]

104 - Abraham Walkowitz, Abstraktion New York, 1912
104 - Abraham Walkowitz, New York Abstraction, 1912

Auch die Philosophie der amerikanischen Naturapologeten Henry David Thoreau und Ralph Waldo Emerson wurzelt in der heftigen Ablehnung der Großstadt:

„You must not count much upon what I can do or learn in New York. I feel a good way off here; and it is not to be visited, but seen and dwelt in... I don't like the city better, the more I see it, but worse. I am ashamed of my eyes that behold it. It is a thousand times meaner than I could have imagined. It will be something to hate, - that's the advantage it will be to me; and even the best people in it are a part of it, and talk coolly about it... When will the world learn that a million men are of no importance compared with one man?"[65] schreibt Thoreau bereits 1843 an Emerson in Vorahnung der noch ins Haus stehenden explosiven Entwicklung der Stadt.

Auf der einen Seite die ‚Apotheose', die Metropole als Menschenwunder, auf der anderen Seite Metaphern wie Sumpf, Dschungel, Vulkan 105-106, Dämon 107, Moloch, Babylon. Sicher liegt die Anziehungskraft der großen Stadt gerade in jener Zerissenheit, jenem Zwiespalt zwischen Faszination und Erschrecken. Er erweist sich als provokativer Nährboden. Und so sind die Gemälde, Gedichte, Romane und Filme, deren Motiv die Großstadt ist, oft die Widerspiegelung einer Mischung aus Haß und Liebe, aus Kritik und Stolz, wie das bereits 1916 in Carl Sandburgs *Chicago Poems* zum Ausdruck kommt:

„CHICAGO 108

Schweinemetzger der Welt,
Werkzeugfabrik, Weizenstapelplatz,
Spieler mit Eisenbahnen, Warenhändler der Nation,
Stürmisch, rauh, lärmend,
Stadt der breiten Schultern:
Sie sagen, du seiest verworfen, und ich glaube ihnen, denn ich sah deine geschminkten Frauen unter Gaslampen Bauernburschen anlocken.
Und sie sagen, du seiest schlecht, und ich antworte: Ja, es ist wahr. Ich sah die Gangster morden und frei umhergehen, um weiter zu morden.
Und sie sagen, du seiest roh, und ich antworte: Auf den Gesichtern der Frauen und Kinder sah ich Spuren lüsternen Hungers.
Und so antwortend, wende ich mich nochmals denen zu, die meiner Stadt spotten, und ich gebe ihnen den Spott zurück und sage:
Kommt und zeigt mir eine andere Stadt, die erhobenen Hauptes singt, so stolz lebt, so wild und stark und schlau..."[66]

105 - John Heartfield, Umschlag: Upton Sinclair: „Der Sumpf", 1928
105 - John Heartfield, Dust Cover: Upton Sinclair "The Jungle", 1928

The philosophy of those great American apologists for nature, Henry David Thoreau and Ralph Waldo Emerson also finds its roots in a strong condemnation of the city:

"You must not count much upon what I can do or learn in New York. I feel a good way off here; and it is not to be visited, but to be seen and dwelt in... I don't like the city better, the more I see it, but worse. I am ashamed of my eyes that behold it. It is a thousand times meaner than I could have imagined. It will be something to hate, - that's the advantage it will be to me; and even the best people in it are part of it, and talk coolly about it... When will the world learn that a million men are of no importance compared with one man?"[65] wrote Thoreau to Emerson in 1843, intuiting the as yet unleashed explosive development of the city.

On the one side we have "apotheosis", the metropolis as the wonder of man, on the other metaphors such as swamp, jungle, volcano 105-106, demon 107, Moloch, Babylon. Surely the power of attraction of the large city lies in precisely this fissure, this conflict between fascination and terror. This is another provocative, fertile ground. And so the paintings, poems, novels and films that have the metropolis as their motif often reflect a mixture of hate and love, of criticism and at the same time pride, as is evident already in Carl Sandberg's *Chicago Poems* of 1916:

106 - Ernst Aufsesser, Schutzumschlag: Bertolt Brecht: „Im Dickicht der Städte", 1927

106 - Ernst Aufsesser, Dust cover: Bertolt Brecht's "In the Thicket of the Cities", 1927

107 - Schutzumschlag: Paul Grulich: „Dämon Berlin. Aufzeichnungen eines Obdachlosen", 1907

107 - Dust cover: Paul Grulich's "Demon Berlin. Writings of a Homeless Person", 1907

108 - Chicago von der Aussichtsterrasse des Hancock Center, 1990
108 - Chicago seen from the observation platform of the Hancock Centre, 1990

CHICAGO [108]

Hog butcher of the world
Tool factory, wheat stacking place,
Player with railroads and the nation's freight handler;
Stormy, husky, brawling,
City of the big shoulders:
They tell me you are wicked and I believe them, for I have seen your painted women under the gas lamps luring the farm boys.
And they tell me you are crooked and I answer:
Yes it is true I have seen the gunmen kill and go free to kill again.
And they tell me you are brutal and my reply is:
On the faces of women and children I have seen the marks of wanton hunger.
And having answered so I turn once more to those who sneer and say to them:
Come and show me another city singing with raised head, so proud to be alive and strong and cunning.[66]

Aus diesem Gedicht spricht nicht nur ganz allgemein das erwachende amerikanische Selbstbewußtsein, sondern ein Stolz und eine Zuneigung, die auf Aneignung basiert. Das Abbilden wird für den Künstler zu einer Art Zähmung. Indem er über die große Stadt schreibt, sie malt, fotografiert, filmt, eignet er sie sich an. Er verarbeitet seine Erfahrungen und rückt der Stadt näher, er assimiliert sich mit ihr, er ergreift Besitz von ihr. 109 Die Metropole wird seine Stadt, ja sozusagen sein persönliches Eigentum. Er nährt sich von ihr und sie sich von ihm, indem er sie abbildet und somit zu ihrer Bekanntheit, zu ihrem Ruhm beiträgt.

„A cruel and brutal city by turns; a callous, money-seeking and unsentimental city, as one looks here and there. But lyric, too. And spendthrift. Frittering, idle, wasteful - saving nothing, hoarding nothing, unless maybe, unmarketable dreams. And dreaming so, even in the face of brutality and calculation. Yet, in the face of this strain, failure, none of its lyric days going unnoted, none of its spell evaded... cannot step out of my door save with a thrill responsive to it all - its grandeur, mystery, glory - yea, Babylonian eternity... ."[67]

This poem reflects not merely the nascent American self-confidence; there is also pride and affection that have their roots in appropriation. The artistic representation becomes a taming process for the artist. In writing, painting, photographing, filming the big city, the artist makes it his own. He works on his experiences and moves nearer to the city, becomes assimilated in it, takes possession of it. 109 The metropolis becomes his city, his personal property, so to speak. By portraying the city and thus contributing to its fame the city nourishes him and he the city.

"A cruel and brutal city by turns; a callous, money-seeking and unsentimental city, as one looks here and there. But lyric, too. And spendthrift. Frittering, idle, wasteful - saving nothing, hoarding nothing, unless maybe, unmarketable dreams. And dreaming so, even in the face of brutality and calculation. Yet, in the face of this strain, failure, none of its lyric days going unnoted, none of its spell evaded... cannot step out of my door save with a thrill responsive to it all - its grandeur, mystery, glory - yea, Babylonian eternity... ."[67]

109 - Martin Weinberg, Schutzumschlag: Seitz, Robert/Zucker, Heinz (Hrsg.): „Um uns die Stadt", 1931
109 - Martin Weinberg, Dust cover: Robert Seitz and Heinz Zuckers (Ed.) „Around Us the City", 1931

Ich und die Stadt

Erst gegen Ende des 19. Jahrhunderts, im Fin de siècle, der Zeit von Symbolismus, Jugendstil und Neuromantik, schärft die Psychoanalyse den Blick für die Mechanismen im psychischen Haushalt des Städters, die von den Wirklichkeitserfahrungen der ihn umgebenden Stadt ausgelöst werden: 110 Im vorher Gesagten habe ich versucht auf das einzugehen, was in folgenden Stichworten zusammenzufassen wäre: beschleunigte Wahrnehmung, erhöhte Reaktionsgeschwindigkeit, abstrakte Kommunikation, Berührungsangst, Aggression, Distanz, Konsumhaltung. In analoger Weise antwortet menschliches Bewußtsein auf die Erfahrungen von Verkehr, Tempo, Medien, Reklame und Industriedesign mit Nervosität und Jargon. 111

110 - Schutzumschlag: Roters, Eberhart/Schulz, Bernard (Hrsg.): „Ich und die Stadt", 1987
110 - Dust cover: Eberhard Roters and Bernard Schultz (Ed.)"I and the City", 1987

The City and I

Towards the end of the nineteenth century - that fin-de-siècle period of Symbolism, Jugendstil and Neo-Romanticism - psychoanalysis generated an awareness of the mechanisms of the city dweller mentality that were specifically triggered by the realities of the city environment: 110 The above could perhaps be summarised in the following key words: accelerated perception and reaction, abstract communication, fear of contact, aggression, distance, consumerism. Human consciousness reacts in a similar way, with nervousness and jargon, to the experiences of traffic, speed, the media, advertising and industrial design. 111

111 - Ludwig Meidner, Ich und die Stadt, 1913
111 - Ludwig Meidner, I and the City, 1913

Und es ist Georg Simmel in seinem Aufsatz *Die Großstädte und ihr Geistesleben,*[68] der die psychologischen und physiologischen Bedingungen des Großstadtmenschen herausstellt. Die menschlichen Reaktionen auf solche Existenzbedingungen nennt er - im völligen Gegensatz zur Kulturkritik des 19. Jahrhunderts und zum Kulturpessimismus des frühen 20. Jahrhunderts - nicht Deformation, sondern notwendige Überlebenstechnik. „Die psychologischen Grundlagen (und dies gilt im besonderen für die Schriftsteller, Maler und Regisseure), auf denen der Typus großstädtischer Individualitäten sich erhebt, ist die Steigerung des Nervenlebens, die aus dem raschen und ununterbrochenen Wechsel äußerer und innerer Eindrücke hervorgeht. 112-113 Der Mensch ist ein Unterschiedswesen, d. h. sein Bewußtsein wird durch den Unterschied des augenblicklichen Eindrucks gegen den vorhergehenden angeregt; beharrende Eindrücke, Geringfügigkeit ihrer Differenzen, gewohnte Regelmäßigkeit ihres Ablaufs und ihrer Gegensätze verbrauchen sozusagen weniger Bewußtsein, als die rasche Zusammendrängung wechselnder Bilder, der schroffe Abstand innerhalb dessen, was man mit einem Blick umfaßt, die Unerwartetheit sich aufdrängender Impressionen. Indem die Großstadt gerade diese psychologischen Bedingungen schafft - mit jedem Gang über die Straße, mit dem Tempo und den Mannigfaltigkeiten des wirtschaftlichen, beruflichen, gesellschaftlichen Lebens - stiftet sie schon in den sinnlichen Fundamenten des Seelenlebens, 114 in dem Bewußtseinsquantum, das sie uns wegen unserer Organisation als Unterschiedswesen abfordert, einen tiefen Gegensatz gegen die Kleinstadt und das Landleben, mit dem langsameren, gewohnteren, gleichmäßiger fließenden Rhythmus ihres sinnlich-geistigen Lebensbildes. Daraus wird vor allem der intellektualistische Charakter des großstädtischen Seelenlebens begreiflich."[69]

112 - UMBO, Der rasende Reporter Egon Erwin Kisch, 1926
112 - UMBO, The Breakneck Reporter Egon Erwin Kisch, 1926

113 - John Heartfield, Es kommt darauf an, wohin die Reise geht, um 1927
113 - John Heartfield, It Always Depends on where the Journey is Leading to, ca. 1927

Georg Simmel sets out the psychological and physiological conditions of the big city dweller in his essay *Die Großstädte und ihr Geistesleben*[68] (The Metropoli and Their Mental Life). The human reactions to such existential conditions are not so much, in his opinion - and in open contradiction of the cultural critiques of the nineteenth century and the cultural pessimism of the early twentieth century - a question of deformation as of survival techniques. "The psychological foundations (and this is especially true of writers, painters and filmmakers) on which typically metropolitan traits are built, involve the increase of nervous life that results from the rapid and continuous changing of internal and external impressions. 112-113 The human being is a distinguishing creature, in other words, his consciousness is excited by the distinctions between present and previous impressions. Persistently occurring impressions, with negligible differences between them, and with habitual regularity in their course and their contrasts, demand, so to speak, less consciousness than the sudden convergence of differing images, the harsh contrasts marking what can be seen at a single glance, the unexpectedness of oncoming impressions. In providing these psychological conditions, with every step taken across the street, with the speed and variety of commercial, professional, social life, it establishes deep down in the material foundations of mental life 114 - in the quantity of consciousness it demands from us because of our organization as distinguishing beings - a profound contrast to small-town or country life with its slower, more routine, steadier-flowing rhythm of mental life. Thus the intellectual character of big city life begins to be comprehensible."[69]

114 - Herbert Bayer, Einsamer Großstädter/Selbstporträt, 1932
114 - Herbert Bayer, Lonely City Dweller/Self Portrait, 1932

Anhand der Berliner Großstadtmalerei sowie anhand von einigen Zitaten, die zeigen, wie das Künstler-Individuum sich in psychischer und physischer Aneignung die Stadt erobert und zu einer - seiner - Existenzbedingung macht, will ich die Provokation der Großstadt, die Steigerung des Nervenlebens, wie Simmel sie nennt, verdeutlichen.

Das Zentrum der Großstadtmalerei im 19. Jahrhundert war Paris, insbesondere das Paris der Impressionisten. Die Großstadtmalerei des 20. Jahrhunderts ist zum größten Teil in Berlin entstanden. 115 Das Motiv hat hier seine stärkste Verdichtung erfahren. Das Berlin der zehner und zwanziger Jahre kann geradezu als energetisches Zentrum dieser Gattung der bildenden Kunst bezeichnet werden, die für das säkulare Epochenbewußtsein zum Erkennungszeichen geworden ist. In der Großstadtmalerei manifestiert sich die Geisteshaltung der europäischen Gesellschaft des 20. Jahrhunderts, in ihr wird sie komprimiert zur Sichtbarkeit gebracht...

115 - Ernst Ludwig Kirchner, Brandenburger Tor, 1929
115 - Ernst Ludwig Kirchner, Brandenburg Gate, 1929

I would like to illustrate the stimulus and provocation of the metropolis - the increase of nervous life, as Simmel puts it - by analysing Berlin paintings of metropolitan themes, as well as by a few quotes that show how individual artists conquer the city, appropriating it physically and psychologically and thus making it a condition of their existence.

The capital of metropolitan painting in the nineteenth century was Paris, especially the Paris of the Impressionists. By the first half of the twentieth century this role had been taken over by Berlin. It is here that themes are to be found in their most condensed form. [115] The Berlin of the second and third decades of the century can be considered the energetic centre of that particular genre in the fine arts which has become a trademark of the secular epoch. It is in the painting of the metropolis that the mentality of European society in the twentieth century manifests itself, is made visible in a compressed form...

Die Berliner Großstadtgesellschaft war noch jung, kaum ihren Kinderschuhen entwachsen, halbwüchsig, naiv, prahlerisch, unternehmungslustig und voller vitaler Neugier, einer Neugier, die durch die Ereignisse des Ersten Weltkrieges zwar ihre Unschuld verloren hatte, 116-117 an Trauma, Trauer und Zynismus gewann, aber daran nicht zugrunde ging, sondern, wenn auch gebrochen, erhalten blieb. 118-119

116 - George Grosz, Grauer Tag, 1921
116 - George Grosz, Grey Day, 1921

117 - Rudolf Schlichter, Hausvogteiplatz, 1926
117 - Rudolf Schlichter, Hausvogteiplatz, 1926

Berlin urban society was at that time still young, had barely reached adolescence, was half-developed, naive, boastful, ready for any venture and full of lively curiosity, a curiosity that lost its innocence with the events of the First World War, 116-117 but gained cynicism, trauma and sadness. It refused to be destroyed, however, but rather survived, albeit in a fractured form. 118-119

118 - George Grosz, Straßenszene, 1923
118 - George Grosz, Street Scene, 1923

119 - George Grosz, Stützen der Gesellschaft, 1926
119 - George Grosz, Pillars of Society, 1926

Die Menschen in den alten Weltstädten Europas stellten sich den geistigen, technischen und sozialen Herausforderungen des 20. Jahrhunderts aus dem Erfahrungswissen jahrhundertelanger großstädtischer Tradition heraus. 120-121 Die Berliner indes begegneten diesen Anforderungen unvermittelt und direkt, sie rannten ohne große Erfahrung in sie hinein. Sie kollidierten mit dem Jahrhundert. Die Berliner Großstadtmalerei 122 ist ein Abbild dieses Zusammenstoßes.[70]

Wim Wenders kommentiert den Zusammenstoß: „Ich brauche die Stadt als meine Existenzbedingung... Da habe ich alles was ich brauche, physisch und psychisch, als Stadt um mich herum.“ Und wie er in einem Interview „Find myself a city to live in...“[71] betonte, war das für ihn Berlin. Für andere ist es New York, Paris oder London.
„In Paris bin ich sehr gern. Wie es Leute hat geben können, die nicht gern hier waren, begreife ich nicht, ich möchte mich jahrelang, ja ein Leben lang hier aufhalten und denke nur mit Entsetzen daran, daß ich wieder werde scheiden müssen. Es ist doch ein ganz anderer Strom auf dem man segelt... Paris ist keine Stadt, sondern eine Welt, wenigstens hat man nirgends so viel auf einmal von der Welt beisammen, wie hier; es ist eben genug, um einen Menschen, der alles auffassen und in seinen Nutzen verwenden möchte, zur Verzweiflung zu bringen.[72] Es ist bei mir wirklich, wenn ich diese Straßen durchwandere, oder in eins dieser weltberühmten Gebäude eintrete, ein zugleich stolzes und demütiges Gefühl, das mich jedesmal erfaßt und sehr oft rufe ich laut aus: Ich freue mich![73] Paris wird immer der Mittelpunkt meiner Wünsche bleiben,“ konstatiert bereits 1843 Christian Friedrich Hebbel.[74]

120 - Ernst Ludwig Kirchner, Drei Straßenmädchen vor Schaufenster, 1914
120 - Ernst Ludwig Kirchner, Three Prostitutes in Front of a Shop Window, 1914

121 - Ernst Ludwig Kirchner, Berliner Straßenzene, 1913
121 - Ernst Ludwig Kirchner, Berlin Street Scene, 1913

The social body of the old grand metropoli of Europe embraced the spiritual, technical and social demands of the century with an open-mindedness born of the wisdom of experience nurtured during hundreds of years of urban tradition. 120-121 Among these, the citizens of Berlin met these demands immediately and directly, lacking experience, they blindly embraced the new. They collided with the century. Berlin city painting 122 is a representation of this collision.[70]

Wim Wenders commented this collision: "I need the city as a condition of my existence... I have everything I need, physically and mentally, in the city around me." And in the interview "Find myself a city to live in..."[71] to him this was Berlin. To others it is New York, Paris, or London.

122 - Richard Ziegler, Vor dem Schaufenster, 1927/28
122 - Richard Ziegler, In Front of the Shop Window, 1927/28

"I really like being in Paris. I can't understand how there can have been people who didn't like being here. I would like to stay here for years, for a lifetime, and I am horrified by the thought of leaving. One sails on a different current... Paris isn't a city, but rather a world; no other place on earth has so much of the world in one place; it is enough to drive to distraction anyone who means to grasp everything and turn it to his advantage...[72] Whenever I wander through the streets or enter one of these world famous buildings I feel at once proud and humiliated, and I often shout out loud: I'm happy![73] Paris will always be the centre of my desires,"

confirmed Christian Friedrich Hebbel as early as 1843.[74]

„In Paris angelangt, war ich endlich imstande, die irgendwie lunarische Freude auszudrücken ... In Paris hatte ich endlich die Vision von dem, was ich erreichen wollte. Ich entdeckte dort eine neue psychische Dimension meiner Malerei und wußte, daß dort meine Heimat war“, schreibt 1928 Marc Chagall.[75] 123-124

Paris. Ma ville ist das gemeinsame Buch von Blaise Cendrars und Fernand Léger betitelt. „Das ist nicht unbedingt Paris. Es ist DIE STADT, die altvertraute Stadt Fernand Légers, vielleicht sogar Argentan, für einen, der, wie er, in der Normandie aufwuchs. Jedenfalls nicht New York, nein keine Metropole. Allerdings ist da der Eiffelturm, auf Zehenspitzen, der sich über die Dächer neigt und eintaucht in die Straße. Es ist also doch Paris, bis auf eine Kleinigkeit, diese Kleinigkeit...“[76] 125-126

Der aristokratische Nomade Rainer Maria Rilke verleiht 1915 - so als wären die in den „Aufzeichnungen des Malte Laurids Brigge“[77] niedergelegten autobiographischen Empfindungen nie beschrieben worden - seiner Adoration für Paris Ausdruck:
„... ich ging die rue de Seine hinauf, so unsäglich wiedersehend... dies ärgste Äußerste, das hier denkbar war, schien mir ein solches Glück zu sein, eine solche an mich versprochene Verschwendung, daß, indem ich diese gewissermaßen zum Nullpunkt des Glückes nahm, mein damaliger Zustand, frei und schauend die Gasse hinaufzugehen, den nächsten, dichten, köstlich konstellierten Carrefour vor mir, daß dieser Zustand, zoviele Grade über dem gesichterten Glück des elendsten Untergangs, von einer Erfülltheit und unwiderruflichen Freude gleichsam erschüttert war und mir eine Einheit des Lebens vorstellte wie sie vielleicht nur die Kindheit zuweilen über einen hat bringen dürfen.“[78]
Über Berlin dagegen gibt er den folgenden Kommentar ab:
„Ich weiß nicht, wie soll man sich vertragen mit dieser unwirschen überall gleichzeitigen Stadt, in der alles fortwährend zu Selbstbewußtsein kommt? ... Es gibt nichts, was Berlin besser bezeichnet, als daß man die, die man sucht entbehren muß und von denen gefunden wird, die man eigentlich nicht suchen würde.“[79]

Zu einem vollkommen anderen Urteil über Berlin, kommt ebenfalls im Jahr 1910 ein Doyen der Architektur des 20. Jahrhunderts, Le Corbusier, damals noch Eduard Jeanneret. In einem Brief an seine Eltern zieht er die Bilanz seines Berlin-Aufenthaltes:

123 - Marc Chagall, Vision von Paris, 1960
123 - Marc Chagall, Vision of Paris, 1960

124 - Marc Chagall, Paris bei Nacht, 1954
124 - Marc Chagall, Paris at Night, 1954

"When I arrived in Paris I was finally able to express my somewhat heavenly joy... In Paris I finally had a vision of what I wanted to achieve. It was there that I discovered a new psychical dimension to my painting and knew that that was where my home was," wrote Marc Chagall.[75] 123-124

Paris. Ma ville is the title of the book by Blaise Cendrars and Fernand Léger. "It is not necessarily Paris. It is THE CITY, the old dependable city of Fernand Léger, like maybe even Argentan for someone who grew up in Normandy like he did. In any case not New York, no, definitely not a metropolis. The Eiffel tower is there, however, standing on tiptoe, bending over rooftops and appearing in the street. So it is Paris after all, except for a detail, that detail..."[76] 125-126

Aristocratically minded traveller Rainer Maria Rilke expressed his adoration for Paris in 1915 - as if the autobiographical impressions in "Aufzeichnungen des Malte Laurids Brigge"[77] had never been written:

"I walked up the rue de Seine so unbelievably regarding again... this utmost extreme, that was thinkable here to me seemed to be such bliss, such a profuseness promised to me, that if I took this in a way for a kind of point zero of my bliss, my former state, walking up the lane freely and gazing, in front of me the next, tight and delicate constellation of a Carrefour, that this state, I say, so many graduations above the certain bliss of the most miserable perdition, was convulsed by a fulfilment and irrevocable joy and presented me with such unity of life, that perhaps only childhood can bring over you."[78]
Whereas he comments on Berlin in 1910:
"I just do not know how to make peace with this gruff, in all places simultaneous city, where everything comes to its own consciousness all the time? There is nothing that signifies Berlin more than the fact that you have to make do without those you are looking for and are always found by the ones you are not really looking for."[79]

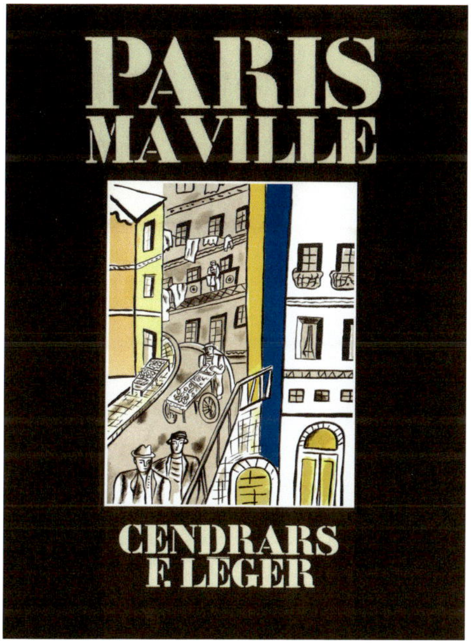

125 - Buchtitel unter Verwendung einer Lithographie (1954) von Fernand Léger
125 - Book cover using a lithograph (1954) of Fernand Léger

126 - Fernand Léger, Gare, (Bahnhof), 1954
126 - Fernand Léger, Railway Station, 1954

„... selten habe ich zehn so anstrengende Tage wie diese verbracht. Ich habe Kilometer und Eindrücke jeglicher Art abgespult. Ich wüßte nicht, wie ich ein einfaches Urteil über Berlin abgeben sollte. Das Schöne mischt sich zum Schrecklichen des infernalen Lebens einer Großstadt. Vielleicht sind die Eindrücke wegen dieser Kontraste stärker. Ich habe das Gefühl das Max(imum) aus diesem kurzen Aufenthalt herausgeholt zu haben.“[80]

Den Prozeß der Entwicklung zum Großstadtmenschen, das Werden eines New Yorkers z.B., beschreibt John Steinbeck in *The Making of a New Yorker*: „From a porthole, then, I saw the city, and there was something monstrous about it - the tall buildings looming to the sky and the lights shining through the falling snow. I crept ashore - frightened and cold and with a touch of panic in my stomach... I stopped to look in a drugstore window where a latex cooch dancer was undulated by a concealed motor - and something burst in my head, a kind of light and a kind of feeling blended into an emotion which if it had spoken would have said, ‚My God! I belong here. Isn't this wonderful?‘ Everything fell into place. I saw every face I passed. I noticed every doorway and the stairways to appartments. I looked across the street at the windows, lace curtains and potted geraniums through sooty glass. It was beautiful - but most important, I was part of it. I was no longer a stranger. I had become a New Yorker.“[81] 127

Belege für diese Faszination, Teil der großen Stadt geworden zu sein, sind zahlreich. „Es lag in Manhattan etwas unerklärlich Erregendes in der Luft, das die Arbeit anstachelte... Die Stadt war geladen mit Eindrücken, und ich brannte von Schaulust.“[82] so George Grosz; und Theodore Dreiser: „It is the city consciousness. Which sees and says: more and more: always more... Nowhere is there anything like it. My city. Not London. Not Paris. Not Moscow. Not any city I have ever seen. So strong, so immense.“[83] Ähnlich hört sich die Hymne an, die Thomas Wolfe in *The Web and the Rock* (1939) der Stadt New York singt: „It is therefore astonishing that nowhere in the world can a young man feel greater hope and expectancy than here. The promise of glorious fulfillment, of love, wealth, fame - or unimaginable joy - is always impending in the air.“[84]

127 - ter Hell, Ich bin's, 1980
127 - ter Hell, It's Me, 1980

In the same year 1910 a completely different opinion is given by one of the great doyens of architecture, Le Corbusier, than Eduard Jeanneret. In a letter to his parents, he characterizes the substance of his stay in Berlin:

"Not in a long time did I spend ten days as strenuous as these last ones. I put miles and impressions of every kind under my belt. I have no idea how to pass a sentence about Berlin that is not highly complex. The Beautiful mixes with the Horrible resulting in the infernal life of a metropolis. Maybe my impressions are stronger for these contrasts. I have the feeling of having extracted the maximum out of this short stay."[80]

The process of becoming a city person, of becoming a New Yorker, for example, is described by John Steinbeck in *The Making of a New Yorker*: "From a porthole, then, I saw the city, and ... there was something monstrous about it - the tall buildings looming to the sky and the lights shining through the falling snow. I crept ashore - frightened and cold and with a touch of panic in my stomach... I stopped to look in a drugstore window where a latex cooch dancer was undulated by a concealed motor - and something burst in my head, a kind of light and a kind of feeling blended into an emotion which if it had spoken would have said, 'My God! I belong here. Isn't this wonderful?' Everything fell into place. I saw every face I passed. I noticed every doorway and the stairways to the apartments. I looked across the street at the windows, lace curtains and potted geraniums through sooty glass. It was beautiful - but most important, I was part of it. I was no longer a stranger. I had become a New Yorker."[81] 127

There are many examples of this excitement at becoming part of the great city. "There was something inexpressibly exciting in the Manhattan air that spurred one to work... The city was loaded with impressions, and I burned with the desire to look,"[82] as George Grosz puts it; and Theodore Dreiser: "It is the city consciousness. Which sees and says: more and more: always more... Nowhere is there anything like it. My City. Not London. Not Paris. Not Moscow. Not any city I have ever seen. So strong, so immense."[83] There is a similar note to the hymn that Thomas Wolfe sings to New York in "The Web and the Rock" (1939): "It is therefore astonishing that nowhere in the world can a young man feel greater hope and expectancy than here. The promise of glorious fulfilment, of love, wealth, fame - or unimaginable joy - is always impending in the air."[84]

Europäische Metropolen im Wandel

The Changing Face of the European Metropolis

Das Wohl und Wehe der europäischen Metropole in einem kurzen Essay abzuhandeln, kommt ein wenig der Tour de force eines überseeischen Besuchers gleich, der sein Europaprogramm in fünf Tagen absolviert. Aus diesem Grunde habe ich meine Fragestellung auf das Phänomen der „urban culture“ und hier wiederum auf drei Einzelaspekte gerichtet. Es sind dies die Fragen nach dem Image und dem Symbolgehalt, nach der Gestaltung - im weitesten Sinne, d.h. politische Entscheidungen miteinbeziehend - und drittens nach der Vermarktung der Stadt. Schnell könnte man zu dem Schluß kommen, daß die Stadt nicht mehr ein Ort zum Wohnen, ein Ort der Kommunikation, der Stimulanz, des Austausches ist, sondern zum Konsumgut, zur Ware degradiert wurde, zu einem Ort, an dem symbolische Ersatzbefriedigung an die Stelle tatsächlicher Bedürfnisbefriedigung getreten ist. Kurz gefaßt könnte man sagen, der Schein tritt an die Stelle des Seins. Die zunehmende Privatisierung, d.h. die auf Grund einer technologischen Vernetzung steigende räumliche und soziale Isolierung, scheint zu einer Abstumpfung gegenüber der individuellen politischen Verantwortung zu führen. Mögliche Folgen des Desinteresses am städtischen Allgemeinwohl wie auch einer kompensatorisch damit einhergehenden Veräußerlichung sind sowohl Provinzialität als auch Borniertheit. Eine städtische Kulturpolitik, die dann noch ihre Entscheidungen einseitig auf ökonomisches Wachstum ausrichtet, d.h. in der die Kultur zur Kulisse degeneriert, ist nicht in der Lage, als geeignetes Gegengewicht eine Beteiligung an und Mitwirkung bei der Gestaltung städtischer Lebensformen zu stimulieren. Ein Gegenbild zu dieser eher pessimistischen Sicht möchte ich am Ende dieses Textes entwickeln.

Hier sei ein kurzer historischer Exkurs gestattet zu dem, was Manuel de Sola Morales im Gegensatz zur Urbanisierung des Landes als „urbane Urbanität“ bezeichnet. Die Funktion von Stadtplanung könnte in diesem Zusammenhang in der Bejahung und Förderung einer städtischen Kultur zu sehen sein. Rückblickend stellt sich die Frage: Gab es früher Formen einer gelungeneren städtischen Kultur, und wenn ja - kann es dann einen Rückgriff auf solche Vorbilder von Urbanität geben? Im Sinne des eben Gesagten muß die Frage nach einer linearen Adaption verneint werden. Dennoch lassen sich aus einer Analyse dessen, was Stadtkultur war, Prinzipien gewinnen, die die heutige Stadtpolitik nicht vernachlässigen oder verletzen sollte.

Vor der Herausbildung der Territorialstaaten war die Stadt ein spezifisches Gemisch aus ökonomischen, politischen und sozialen Strukturen, das in Kontrast zum agrarisch-feudalen Land stand. Urbanität war nicht nur eine Lebens-, sondern auch eine Gesellschaftsform.

In dem Maße, wie sich im Verlauf des Übergangs von der vorindustriellen zur industriellen Zeit die ökonomischen Formen, die bislang stadtspezifisch waren, als kapitalistische Kolonisierung auf alle Wirtschaftsbereiche - also auch auf die Agrarwirtschaft - ausbreiteten, wurde diese spezifische Stadtkultur nach und nach in Europa und Nordamerika zur Form der gesamten Gesellschaft. Die Folge war eine explosive Verstädterung. Gleichzeitig traten in den städtischen Agglomerationen des Industriezeitalters mehrere neue Urbanitäten an die Stelle der einen urbanen Identität - im wesentlichen zwei, die bürgerliche und die proletarische: städtische Kulturen, die sich nun in der Stadt und in der Politik wie Feinde auf dem Schlachtfeld gegenüberstehen.

„Zum Sinnbild und Inbegriff urbanen Verhaltens des ökonomisch selbständigen Bürgertums werden Konsum und Freizeit, intellektuelle Aufgeregtheit und Sensation“ schreiben Hartmut Häußermann und Walter Siebel in ihrem Buch über die „Neue Urbanität.“[1] Geprägt von Not und Solidarität und gestützt durch sozialistische Theorien hat sich auf der anderen Seite als spezifisch städtisches Phänomen im 19. Jahrhundert eine proletarische Kultur entwickelt, die dem Proletariat ein Bewußtsein und Selbstbewußtsein gegeben hat, ohne das sie schlicht passive Armutskultur geblieben wäre.

To consider the highs and the lows of the European metropolis over the space of a couple of pages resembles to me a little bit the typical experience of a non-European visitor's "European highlights in five days"-program ending in a slide-sorting chaos two month after coming back home.
It is for that reason that I have decided to concentrate my remarks on the field of "urban culture" and three of its basic aspects, especially in those plans and planning decisions that are displayed in them. They consist of the quest for image and symbolic context as well as urban design in the widest possible sense - and this of course includes political decisions - and finally for the "marketing" of cities.

Quickly we could thus arrive at the conclusion that a city is not any more: a place to live in, a base for communication, a platform for stimulation or exchange, but that it is degenerating into an object of consumption, a purchasable good; that it has become the lieu of symbolic "ersatz" - satisfaction instead of a place that really satisfies existing needs. To put it short one could say that appearances have replaced real being.
Growing privatisation - here seen as social and spatial isolation resulting from the growth of technological networks - seems to lead towards a negation of individual political responsibility.
Possible results of a lack of general interest in urban well-being as well as its compensatory replacement by superficial activities all lead to provincialism and narrow-mindedness.
If on top of that urban cultural policy aims its decisions exclusively at the target of economic growth by using cultural matters as mere ornamentation, it will not any more be in a position from which it can stimulate participation in or responsibility for qualitative urban forms of life as a balance.

Near the end of my essay, I will try to give a different vision opposing the primarily pessimistic remarks of this opening, but first allow me a short historical digression to what Manuel de Solar Morales of Barcelona calls 'urban urbanity' as opposed to an urbanization of the country. Looking back means putting the question whether there were historically successful attempts at urban culture, and if so, whether we today can usefully employ such models of urbanity.
In the light of what we have seen before, the possibility of a linear adaptation has to be negated. Nevertheless we can gain out of an analysis of the elements of former urban cultures some principles that should not be neglected or violated by today's urban policies.

In the era before the forming of territorial political units (duchies and kingdoms), a town or a city was a specific mixture of economic, political and social structures in distinct contrast to the feudally organized countryside.
Urbanity was not only a way of life but also a social system. During the transformation from pre-industrial to industrial times economic structures, which heretofore were characteristic to urban life, spread by a process of capitalistic colonisation across all areas of economic activity. That included also agrarian production, thus eliminating an especially urban culture and generally became the basic structure of social life in Europe as well as North America.
As a consequence we have an explosive urbanization process both socially - defined as a fundamental change in ways of life - and topographically through growth of existing and founding of new cities.

Geld und Zeit waren die Voraussetzung, um das Kauf- und Kulturangebot und die sich stets raffinierter gestaltenden Sensationen wahrnehmen zu können oder sie gar selbst mitzugestalten. Die Befreiung von notwendiger Lohnarbeit und die Entbindung von den Lasten täglicher Reproduktionsarbeit waren die Voraussetzung dieser städtischen und bürgerlichen Kultur, von der das Proletariat und das Kleinbürgertum ausgeschlossen waren. Walter Ruttmann zeigt in seinem 1927 entstandenen Film „Berlin. Die Sinfonie der Großstadt“[2] auf äußerst beeindruckende Art und Weise das Nebeneinander dieser Urbanitäten, deren Verlust und Auflösung wir heute beklagen.

Städtische Kultur, die sich bis zum Zweiten Weltkrieg noch aus dem Nebeneinander oder der Polarität von bürgerlichen und proletarischen Werthaltungen bestimmte, hat ihre gesellschaftspolitische Perspektive inzwischen verloren. Darüber hinaus haben die politischen Emanzipationsbewegungen der Arbeiter durch die einseitige Konzentration auf die Fragen des Produktionsbereiches sich anderer politisch brisanter Themen nicht mehr angenommen. Von den Konzeptionen der utopischen Sozialisten bis zur Wohnungsbaupolitik der europäischen Nationen in den 50er bis 90er Jahren des vorigen Jahrhunderts hat sich der gesellschaftspolitische Gehalt der Stadtpolitik zunehmend reduziert. Die Abwendung der Arbeiterbewegung von den Fragen der Wohnungs- und Stadtplanung, von den Fragen der Stadtpolitik und der Organisation des Alltags hat seit dem 19. Jahrhundert wesentlich zu ihrer Entpolitisierung beigetragen. Diese politische Betroffenheit als Teil der städtischen Kultur, als Bestandteil der Urbanität wieder zu beleben, wäre eine Aufgabe sowohl für die Gewerkschaften als auch für die politischen Parteien.

So wie sich das Kleinbürgertum und das Proletariat als emanzipierte und verantwortliche Träger städtischer Kultur disqualifiziert haben, hat dies auch das Bürgertum getan. Bürgerliche Urbanität war historisch an die Stadt gebunden: ökonomisch als Markt-Oikomene gegenüber der ländlichen Oikos-Wirtschaft, politisch als Frühform der Demokratie gegen feudalistische Herrschaftsstrukturen und kulturell in der Dialektik zwischen Öffentlichkeit und Privatheit und in der Befreiung von der sozialen Kontrolle der dörflichen Nachbarschaft.

Mit der Integration bürgerlich-städtischer Politik in die Politik der Territorialstaaten hat die bürgerliche Urbanität ihren noch zu Beginn des 19. Jahrhunderts existierenden politisch-emanzipatorischen Gehalt verloren.
Die bürgerliche Dialektik von Privatheit und Öffentlichkeit ist zu einem Gegenüber von Kaufen und Verbrauchen verkommen.
In diesem Sinne kann von einem Verfall der städtischen Lebensform als politischer Kultur gesprochen werden. Woran jedoch soll ein Stadtbewohner angesichts der ökonomischen Prämissen von Wachstum und Schrumpfen sein urbanes Selbstbewußtsein festmachen, woran soll ein Politiker seine Stadtentwicklungspolitik orientieren, worauf soll Stadtplanung Bezug nehmen? Ich komme hier auf das Problem von Image, Gestalt und Vermarktung der Stadt zurück. Und ich frage: Wie weit entspricht das Image, welches ein Politiker von seiner Stadt entwirft, der Realität? Was meint ein Slogan, der Rotterdam ein „Manhattan an der Maas“ nennt? Wird auf die Stadtsilhouette von downtown New York Bezug genommen, auf die Grund- und Bodenpreise, auf die Monofunktionalität eines metropolitanen Areals, welches vorrangig dem tertiären und quartären Sektor dient? Sicherlich wünscht man sich in Rotterdam nicht die Assoziation mit nahezu hunderttausend New Yorker Obdachlosen,[3] die dennoch Resultat ein und derselben Politik sind, der auch New Yorks Stadtteil Manhattan seine spezifische Existenz verdankt.

At the same time within urban agglomerations of the industrial period the urban entity is supplanted by a group of urban cultural patterns - mainly the bourgeois and proletarian forms of life - cultural patterns opposed in the city itself as well as in politics as enemies on the battlefield. "Consumption and leisure time become symbol and essence of the urban life of the economically independent middle classes as well as the intellectual agitation and sensation," Hartmut Häußermann and Walter Siebel wrote in their book on "New Urbanism" ("Neue Urbanität").[1]
On the other hand in the nineteenth century a proletarian culture has grown out of the experience of need and therefore the necessity to find forms of solidarity. The process was aided by the formulation of socialist theories as a specifically urban phenomenon, which gave awareness and self-consciousness to a proletariat that otherwise would have remained within the boundaries of a passive culture of poverty.
Time and money were the necessary prerequisites to be able to respond to a growing variety of selling and purchasing and to cultural opportunities that grew to be more and more refined every day - or even to actively have a say in their shaping. Liberation from the necessity to work for wages, being freed from the weight of daily reproduction labour were preconditions of the urban and middle class culture, from which the proletariat and petit bourgeoisie were excluded.
Walter Ruttmann's 1927 movie "Berlin, the Symphony of the Metropolis," "Berlin, die Sinfonie der Großstadt,"[2] very expressively shows the side-by-side existence of the widely different urban ways of varying lifestyles, the loss and extinction of which we mourn today.

Urban culture that up to the Second World War still was defined by the polarity and coexistence of middle class and proletarian values, meanwhile lost its sociological perspective.

On the one hand, the worker's politically emancipating movements through their one-sided concentration on the question of production conditions have excluded other politically explosive topics. Since the concepts of the utopian socialists, the public housing policy of the European nations during the 1950ies, 60ies, 70ies, 80ies and 90ies of the last century sociopolitical context of urban strategies have continuously thinned out.
The estrangement however of the worker's movement from the issues of housing and urban policy, from town-planning problems and the organization of everyday-life since the 19th century contributed essentially to its de-politicising.
To rekindle this political interest as part of an urban culture by rights should constitute a task for trade unions and political parties.

In the same way as proletariat and petit bourgeoisie, the middle classes have failed as emancipated and responsible participants in urban culture.
Middle-class-urbanity historically was linked to the city: economically as market-'oikomenae' as opposed to the rural 'oikos'-economy of self-subsistence; politically as precursor of democracy against feudal structures of power; culturally as the dialectic opposition of public and private sphere against the social control of a village-neighbourhood.
Along with the integration of middle-class-urban policies into the policy of the emerging territorial empires the bourgeois way of urban life lost its - at the beginning of the 19th century still existing - political emancipating effect.
The middle-class dialectic of privacy and public sphere has degenerated into an opposition between selling and consuming.
In this context we can assume a degeneration of urban ways of life as political culture.
Where can the citizen anchor his urban self-consciousness in the face of economic processes like growth and recession; on what does the politician base his urban development-concept, what reference is still valid for town-planning strategies?

Imagebildung scheint heute kein Prozeß mehr zu sein. Ein Image entsteht nicht mehr im Laufe der Zeit. Es wird entworfen, konzipiert.[4] Das Bild von einer Stadt, ihre Reputation, entsteht nicht mehr auf Grund der tatsächlichen Qualitäten und charakteristischen Prägungen, sondern wird als Marketingprodukt geschaffen. Die Werbeagentur souffliert eine intakte städtische Maschinerie und antizipiert, daß der Investor oder der Ansiedler sie sich so wünscht, die „brainparks" und „media parks" etc., und das obwohl sich selbst renommierte Prognose-Institute zurückhalten, wenn es darum geht, Dynamik und Reichweite des technischen Fortschrittes vorauszusagen.

Im Rahmen des interkommunalen Konkurrenzkampfes sind nahezu alle Gemeinden an einer Stärkung ihres Images interessiert. Hier haben die Metropolen zweifellos Vorteile. In ihr Image sind historische Bedeutsamkeiten genauso wie besondere stadträumliche Qualitäten bereits inkorporiert. Sie zehren einerseits von dem metropolitanen Glorienschein, der sie seit dem 19. Jahrhundert umgibt. Metropolis, das heißt in seiner etymologischen Bedeutung die „Mutterstadt", die besondere urbs, die als Ort des Vorlebens, des Experiments, als Schauplatz für „variety" und „multitude", die anderen Städte auf den zweiten Rang verweist. Metropolis wird gern auch als eine Art Beschwörungsformel für die Vermarktung von Stadtagglomerationen wie die niederländische „randstad" oder das Ruhrgebiet herbeizitiert, oder als Adjektiv zur Aufwertung von Firmen, Büros und Institutionen jedweder Art dem jeweiligen Namen hinzugefügt, um sich wenigstens verbal gegenüber dem Alltäglichen und Provinziellen hervorzuheben.

Neben den sich allgemein an die Metropole knüpfenden Assoziationen, Erwartungen und Hoffnungen hat andererseits jede europäische Metropole noch ihre eigene Symbolkraft. Meist wird ein einziges Bauwerk zum Symbolträger par excellence. Weltweit weiß man sofort, daß mit der Wiedergabe des Eiffelturms Paris, mit der des Brandenburger Tores Berlin gemeint ist. Deshalb ist es verständlich, daß die Städte bei ihrem politischen und planerischen Handeln auf die architektonische und stadträumliche Gestaltung zur Stärkung ihres Images zurückgreifen.

Einige Städte - und hier wiederum insbesondere die Metropolen - bewegen sich heute noch in einer jahrhundertelangen Tradition, was ihre Planungsentscheidungen angeht. Die „grande geste", mit der französische Ministerpräsidenten - hießen sie nun Mitterand oder Pompidou - ihre Kapitale gestalteten, liegt in einer Linie mit den Gestaltungsvorstellungen eines Henri IV., Louis XIV. oder Napoleon III. Welche urbane Kultur und welche Träger dieser Kultur sich noch bis zu den Aktivitäten des Baron Eugene Haussmann in den Monumentaleingriffen und Bauten spiegeln, ist eindeutig. Wen aber und was repräsentieren die Pariser Großprojekte heute?

Zweifelsfrei sind sie Produkte einer urbanen Kultur, wie alle städtischen Herzeige-Architekturen. Sie sollen der Attraktivitätssteigerung und Imagestärkung dienen. Nicht nur spektakuläre Repräsentationsbauten, sondern auch die Ästhetik im allgemeinen, die Kultur und die Geschichte werden als Standortfaktoren instrumentalisiert.

„Stadtbaukultur" erweist sich im Sinne der politischen Dimension des Urbanen jedoch nicht nur in der Produktion von Kronjuwelen, sondern auch in der Bewältigung von alltäglichen und gewöhnlichen Bau- und Planungsaufgaben.

Here I would like to return to the question of the image, shape and marketing of towns. I want to ask: how far does the image that the politician - mostly aiming at the marketing strategy for his town - presents of his community reflect reality? What does it mean if PR-professionals call Rotterdam: "Manhattan on the Maas" or Frankfurt is selling her image as "Manhattan on Main"? Does the silhouette of Down-Town-New York reflect real-estate costs or the mono-functionality of a metropolitan area which mainly serves tertiary or quaternary functions? Surely Rotterdammers do not strive for association with New York's nearly two hundred thousand homeless[3] - results of the same policy that led to Manhattan's growth.

The forming of an urban image today no longer seems to be a process. An image does not grow anymore, it is designed.[4] The image of a city, its reputation, no longer derives from its factual qualities and characteristic features, it is shaped as a marketing strategy for selling purposes. Advertising agencies suggest a clinical urban machinery and anticipate the investor's or future citizen's imagined concepts, although even reputed prognostication-institutes hesitate to predict the scope and dynamism of technological progress.
Each European metropolis sports at least one or two symbolical "power packs" besides exploiting all the associations, expectations and hopes that are linked to its name. In most cases a building is made a symbolic carrier of significance. Around the world the Eiffel Tower serves as a synonym for Paris, as the Brandenburg Gate stands as a token for Berlin, as does the Tower Bridge for London, etc. Therefore it is easy to understand that cities refer to architectural and town-planning activities when acting in the political or economical field to strengthen their image.

In this game metropolitan cities certainly have an advantage. Historical importance as well as qualities of urban spaces are deeply incorporated into their public image. They feed on the metropolitan glory that surrounds their history from old. "Metropolis" according to the etymologic derivation still means "town of the mother", the special "urbs" that puts other cities into second place concerning its role as model-place of experiment, variety or multitude. Even agglomerations of cities such as Holland's Randstad or Germany's Ruhrgebiet use the term metropolis to conjure up a positive image. Firms, offices or associations of all kinds like it as an escape-route out of everyday provincial limitations.
Some cities and amongst those again the metropolises today are entrapped in some kind of century old traditions concerning their planning decisions. "The grande geste" with which French presidents - be it Pompidou or Mitterand - shaped their capital aligns with planning ideas and decrees of a Henri IV, Louis XIV or Napoleon III.
What kind of urban culture was mirrored in the monumental changes of the structure of the French metropolis by Eugene Baron Haussmann is clear. But who and what is represented by the large-scale-projects: the so called "grands projects" of contemporary Paris? Without doubt they constitute products of an urban culture like all show-off-architectures. They are meant to increase the attractiveness and improve the cities' and the founder's image. Not only spectacular public buildings but also aesthetic features generally, as well as culture and cultural history are employed as arguments for specific locations.

Einerseits ist zu begrüßen, daß die Städte sich selbstbewußt der eigenen Geschichte sowie ästhetischen Fragen widmen, andererseits sind aber auch restaurative Tendenzen zu kritisieren, in denen Geschichte auf Nostalgie und bauliche Kulissenelemente, Denkmalpflege auf Stadtbild-„Verschönerung" reduziert wird, Stadtbaukunst also zur bloßen Verhübschung gerät. In der Folge werden vielfältig genutzte öffentliche Räume durch „gestaltende Möblierung" im Sinne einer falsch verstandenen architektonischen „Aufwertung" zu kosmetisch behandelten, nahezu sterilen Stadträumen. Dem spezifischen Ort und den Bedürfnissen seiner Bewohner angemessene öffentliche Räume, wie in Barcelona die großen und kleinen Stadtplätze oder in New York die zum Teil winzigen „open spaces" heben sich als Orte des Stadtgebrauches hiervon wohltuend ab.[5]

An dieser Stelle erhebt sich erneut die Frage nach dem Selbstverständnis und dem Einfluß des öffentlichen Bauherrn. Welche Verfahren wählt er, um Planungsentscheidungen qualitativ abzusichern? Welche Prämissen setzt er im Spannungsfeld sozialer, ökonomischer, ökologischer und kultureller Belange? Ein ideales Beispiel aus dem breiten Spektrum einer ausgewogenen Stadtplanungspolitik ist das von mir oft zitierte Baugenehmigungsverfahren für den Warenhauskonzern Karstadt im Berlin der späten 1920er Jahre.[6] Martin Wagner, der damalige Stadtbaurat, gestattete dem Investor das Überschreiten der zulässigen Bauhöhe nur auf der Basis einer Gegenleistung für die Stadt insgesamt. Der Konzern, dem die Niederlassung in der Weltstadt, in der Metropole, ein wichtiges Anliegen war, willigte ein, im Berliner Hinterland ein Feriendorf für Kinder aus den Arbeiterbezirken zu errichten und für den Zeitraum von fünfzig Jahren zu unterhalten. Eine derart offensive Politik, die die ökonomischen Vorteile für den Investor direkt an soziale Verpflichtungen koppelt, sucht man heute vergebens.

The culture of town-planning - the culture of urbanism - in the light of political strategies not only consists of the procurement of crown jewels, but much more in the mastering of every-day-planning and building problems.

On the one hand one has to appreciate that cities become aware of their cultural and aesthetic identity, on the other hand one has to criticise restorative tendencies, that reduce history to nostalgic or architectural set-pieces, and degrade the care for historic monuments into the mere cultivation of the townscape or the art of building cities into the polishing of down-town areas; instead of supporting characteristic every-day sites for the metropolitan inhabitant.

As a consequence manifold usable public spaces degenerate through wrongly applied architectural "improvements" into sterile inner urban zones. Public spaces that are carefully adapted to their specific localization and to the needs of the inhabitants, like examples in Barcelona or New York show, form a welcome contrast as part of the city experience.[5]

This is the moment to raise the question for the public-investor's self - interpretation and influence. By what means does he guarantee the quality of planning decisions? What is his possibility to move in a minefield of social, economic, ecologic or cultural issues? A very apt example I would like to quote out of the wide spectrum of a balanced town-planning strategy is the building-permit policy concerning the department-store-concern of Karstadt in the Berlin of the late 1920ies.[6]

Martin Wagner, then planning officer of the city, gave the investor permission to go beyond the normally permitted heights of construction on the base of a compensation bargain. The concern of Karstadt, striving to be represented in the expanding metropolis - in this case in the South-eastern district of Neukölln - consented to the compensatory construction of holiday-villages for needing Berlin children on the town's periphery and also to their upkeep for no less than fifty years. Today one would look in vain for examples of such an aggressive policy in favour of public benefit, combining the economical advantage of the investor with social obligations for the city. On the contrary - in Berlin shortly after the fall of the wall highly attractive territories of the city at Potsdamer Platz have been sold for incredibly low sums to private investors.

I have mentioned the image making, shaping and marketing of cities. The latter not only signifies the presentation of a gift-wrapped city image to the investor, but also a generally understood way of presenting and explaining means and aims of town-planning ideas and strategies to everybody.

Image, Gestalt und Vermarktung habe ich angesprochen. Mit letzterem meine ich nicht nur die für den Investor werbewirksam verpackte Stadt, sondern ich meine auch die jedem verständliche Vermittlung und Präsentation von städtebaulichen und architektonischen Ideen und Lösungen in dem Sinne, wie es Maurizio Marcelloni formuliert: Nur durch wiederholte und bereits in der Schule 128 vermittelte Informationen über die bauliche und soziale Umwelt läßt sich eine verantwortungsvolle Haltung zur Stadt entwickeln. Jenseits der Vielfalt, der „variety" und „multitude", ist Stadtkultur auch Widerspruch und Konflikt, mit denen Städter wie Politiker umzugehen lernen müssen.

So verspricht städtische Lebensform zwar Entlastung, garantiert die Maschine Stadt das, was Karl Kraus von ihr erwartet: „Ich verlange von der Stadt, in der ich leben soll: Asphalt, Straßenspülung... Luftheizung... Wasserleitung."[7] Sie verlangt aber auch das Aushalten von Ambivalenzen. Aushalten von Ambivalenz heißt aber immer auch Zukunft anstreben, Zukunft gestalten wollen, Möglichkeiten einer sinnvollen Koexistenz suchen. „Wenn es aber Wirklichkeitssinn gibt, und niemand wird bezweifeln, daß er seine Daseinsberechtigung hat, dann muß es auch etwas geben, das man Möglichkeitssinn nennen kann. Wer ihn besitzt, sagt beispielsweise nicht: Hier ist dies oder das geschehen, wird geschehen, muß geschehen, sondern er erfindet: Hier könnte, sollte oder müßte geschehen."[8]

Und wenn ich diesen Gedanken Robert Musils weiterspinne, muß ich nicht nur fragen, ob Planung das wirklich Richtige tut, sondern ob sie gegebenenfalls auch rückgängig zu machen ist. Revidierbarkeit und ironischer Möglichkeitssinn sind eine notwendige Bereicherung der Stadtkultur. Mehr als am sturen Festhalten am Beschluß zeigt sich in ihr die emanzipierte Stadtplanung.

128 - Learning from the city
128 - Learning from the city

Maurizio Marcelloni points this out in an article "Looking at Spain": "We are seeing a strong advertising capacity of the public administrations from official publications to summaries and brochures distributed down to the last capillary vein of society."

Only through repeated information early at school 128 about social and architectural environment a responsible attitude towards urbanity and urban processes is to be generated. Beyond the variety and multitude, urban culture also comprises conflicts and contradictions. They are to be recognized by citizens as well as politicians.

Thus the urban way of life promises relief and can guarantee what Karl Kraus expected from it. "I ask of the city in which I am to live: asphalt, the cleaning of streets ... central heating... running hot water"[7] - but he also expects the toleration of ambivalence and controversy, which in turn leads to the ability to shape the future, to look for possibilities of a meaningful coexistence: "If there exists a sense for reality, there also has to be a sense for possibility... who possesses it for example does not say: here this or that happened, will happen, has to happen, but invents: here could, should, ought to happen."[8]

And if may I develop this motif of Robert Musil: I am not only to ask if planning processes achieve the right thing, but, if the occasion arises, whether one is able to undo its effects. Reversibility as well as an ironically applied sense of opportunity are necessary elements of urban culture. In this - much sooner than in stupidly clinging to decisions made in different circumstances - an emancipated model of urban planning manifests itself.

Anmerkungen „Mythos Metropolis“

[1] Corboz, André: Die Geschichte des Städtebaus als Bedeutungsforschung, in: „archithese“ 2, 1982, S. 43–47

[2] „Time“ Magazine, 11. Januar, 1993, 24/25. Im „Über das Mögliche Hinausdenken“ betitelten Nachwort zur Zweitauflage meines Buches: Architekturkonzeptionen der Utopischen Sozialisten, Berlin 1991, wird diese Frage andiskutiert. 2002 thematisierte Paul Virilio in der Ausstellung ‚Unknown Quantity‘ (Fondation Cartier pour l'art contemporain Paris) die Ambivalenz zwischen Apokalypse, Fortschritt und Hoffnung. Ausstellungskatalog London 2003. Siehe auch: Redman, Chris: Are cities good for us. Buchrezension von John Readers Buch „Cities“, New York 2004. In: „Time“ Magazine 30. August 2004. S. 70/71

[3] Helms, Hans G.: Die Stadt als Gabentisch. Beobachtungen zwischen Manhattan und Berlin Marzahn, Leipzig 1992

[4] George Grosz zitiert in: Riha, Karl: Nachwort zu: George Grosz: New York, hrsg. von Walter Huder und Karl Riha, Siegen 1985, S. 44/45

[5] Wenders, Wim: The act of seeing. Essays, Reden und Gespräche, Frankfurt am Main 1992, S. 128

[6] Nadolny, Sten: Die Entdeckung der Langsamkeit, München 1983

[7] Wenders, Wim: Op.cit., S. 124

[8] Ibidem

[9] Ibidem

[10] Lüdi, Toni und Heidi: Räume für den Film, in: „archithese“ 5, 1992, 47

[11] Wenders, Wim: Op. cit., S. 123

[12] Op.cit., S. 145

[13] Rilke, Rainer Maria: Schriften in Prosa, Zweiter Teil. Die Aufzeichnungen des Malte Laurids Brigge, Leipzig 1930, S. 57–59

[14] Tucholsky, Kurt: Häuser, in: Seitz, Robert/ Zucker, Heinz (Hrsg.): Um uns die Stadt. Eine Anthologie neuer Großstadtdichtung, Berlin 1931, S. 129. Neuauflage hrsg. von Ulrich Conrads, Braunschweig und Wiesbaden 1986

[15] Butor, Michel: Die Stadt als Text. Aus dem französischen (La ville comme texte) von Helmut Scheffel, Graz und Wien 1992, S. 9

[16] Wenders, Wim: Op. cit., S. 120

[17] Piranesi, Giovanni Battista: Invenzioni Capric di Carceri, ca. 1745; ders.: Antichità Romane, 4 Bde, Rom 1756; ders.: Il campo Marzio dell' Antica, Rom 1762. Vgl. hierzu auch: Höper, Corinna (Hrsg.): Giovanni Battista Piranesi, Ausstellungskatalog, Staatsgalerie Stuttgart 1999

[18] Mercier, Louis-Sébastien: Tableaux de Paris, Hamburg/Neuchâtel 1781, 2 Bde.; Amsterdam 1782-1788, Paris 1947 (Ausz.). Übersetzungen: Paris ein Gemählde, B.G. Walch, Leipzig 1783-1784, 8 Bde. - Schilderung von Paris, S.G. Bürde, Breslau 1785. - Neuestes Gemälhde von Paris für Reisende und Nichtreisende, H.A.O. Reichard, Leipzig 1789-1790, 2 Bde. - Paris am Vorabend der Revolution, G. Metgen, Karlsruhe 1967 (m. Vorw.) Benutzte Ausgabe; Mercier, Louis-Sébastien: Tableau de Paris ou explications de différentes figures, gravées à l'eau forte, pour servir au differentes éditions du tableau de Paris, Yverdon 1787, Deutsche Ausgabe: Bilder der Großstadt in Radierungen von Balthasar Anton Dunker. Nebst Erläuterungen, die auf die nämlichen Kapitel im Werk von Louis-Sébastien Mercier verweisen, Neuauflage Berlin 1989, herausgegeben von Paul Thiel.

Notes "The Myth of the Metropolis"

[1] Corboz, André: Die Geschichte des Städtebaus als Bedeutungsforschung, in: "archithese" 2, 1982, pp. 43–47

[2] "Time" Magazine, 11 January, 1993, 24/25. This issue is touched upon in the epilogue "Über das Mögliche Hinausdenken" in the second edition of my book: Architekturkonzeptionen der Utopischen Sozialisten, Berlin 1991. Paul Virilio thematised the ambivalence between apocalypse, progress and hope in 2002 in the exhibition 'Unknown Quantity' (Fondation Cartier pour l'art contemporain, Paris). Exhibition catalogue London 2003. See as well: Redmann, Chris: Are cities good for us. Review of John Reader's book "Cities", New York 2004. In "Time" Magazine, August 30th 2004, pp.70/71

[3] Helms, Hans G.: Die Stadt als Gabentisch. Beobachtungen zwischen Manhattan und Berlin Marzahn, Leipzig 1992

[4] George Grosz quoted in: Riha, Karl: Epilogue: George Grosz: New York, ed. by Walter Huder and Karl Riha, Siegen 1985, pp. 44-45

[5] Wenders, Wim: The act of seeing. Essays, Reden und Gespräche, Frankfurt am Main 1992, p. 128

[6] Nadolny, Sten: Die Entdeckung der Langsamkeit, Munich 1983

[7] Wenders, Wim: op. cit., p. 124

[8] Ibidem

[9] Ibidem

[10] Lüdi, Toni und Heidi: Räume für den Film, in: "archithese" 5, 1992, p. 47

[11] Wenders, Wim: op. cit., p. 123

[12] Op. cit., p. 145

[13] Rilke, Rainer Maria: The Notebooks of Malte Laurids Brigge. Translated by John Lonton. London 1930, p. 45 ff.

[14] Tucholsky, Kurt: Häuser, in: Seitz, Robert/Zucker, Heinz (ed.): Um uns die Stadt. Eine Anthologie neuer Großstadtdichtung, Berlin 1931, p. 129. New edition ed. by Ulrich Conrads, Brunswick and Wiesbaden 1986

[15] Butor, Michel: Die Stadt als Text. Translated from the French (La ville comme texte) by Helmut Scheffel, Graz and Vienna 1992, p. 9

[16] Wenders, Wim: op. cit., p. 120

[17] Piranesi, Giovanni Battista: Invenzioni Capric di Carceri, ca. 1745; idem: Antichità Romane, 4 vols., Rome 1756; idem.: Il campo Marzio dell' Antica, Rom 1762. Cf. also: Höper, Corinna (ed.): Giovanni Battista Piranesi, Exhibition Catalogue, Staatsgalerie Stuttgart 1999

[18] Mercier, Louis-Sébastien: Tableaux de Paris, Hamburg/Neuchâtel 1781, 2 vols.; Amsterdam 1782-1788, Paris 1947 (Exc.). Translations: Paris ein Gemählde, B.G. Walch, Leipzig 1783-1784, 8 vols. - Schilderung von Paris, S.G. Bürde, Breslau 1785. - Neuestes Gemälde von Paris für Reisende und Nichtreisende, H.A.O. Reichard, Leipzig 1789-1790, 2 vols. - Paris am Vorabend der Revolution, G. Metgen, Karlsruhe 1967 (with an introduction) edition used; Mercier, Louis-Sébastien: Tableau de Paris ou explications de différentes figures, gravées à l'eau forte, pour servir au differentes éditions du tableau de Paris, Yverdon 1787, German reference: Bilder der Großstadt in Radierungen von Balthasar Anton Dunker. With comments referring to the relevant chapters in Louis-Sébastien Mercier's work, new edition Berlin 1989, ed. by Paul Thiel

[19] Konrád, György: Die Herausforderung der Großstadt, in: Berner, Peter/Brix, Emil/Mantel, Wolfgang (Hrsg.): Wien um 1900. Aufbruch der Moderne, Wien 1986, S. 259-275

[20] Mercier, Louis-Sébastien: Op. cit., Kapitel DL XXXV, S. 82

[21] Rivarol, zitiert nach Kindlers Literatur Lexikon, Bd. 21, München 1974, S. 9197

[22] Queneau, Raymond: Zazie dans le métro, Paris 1959; Filmfassung: Zazie dans le métro, Frankreich 1960, Regie: Louis Malle. Buch: Louis Malle und Jean Paul Rappenau nach einem Roman von Raymond Queneau, 93 Minuten, Uraufführung 20.12.1960. Die absurde Welt der Erwachsenen, gesehen mit den Augen eines frühreifen Kindes. Die kleine Zazie entdeckt 36 Stunden lang Paris; die Metropole zeigt sich als Großstadtdschungel voller Helden, Bösewichter und Clowns, voller lustiger und makabrer Ereignisse. Nach einem Roman von Queneau inszenierte Louis Malle eine groteske Kinokomödie, wobei er den Sprachwitz der Vorlage konsequent in Bilder zu übersetzen versuchte. Wie der Autor sich mit der scheinbaren Naivität der Kindersprache auseinandersetzt, so kehrt auch Malle in die Kindertage der Kinematographie zurück: zum Slapstick der Mack-Sennet-Filme und zu den Urtricks von Meliès, Zeitlupe, Zeitraffer, Wiederholung und Deformierung, Aufhebung von Raum und Zeit. Spiel mit farblichen Verfremdungen und bewußt falsches Synchronisieren sind zugleich intellektuelle Verballhornungen der Konvention, die den Film zu einem beispielhaften Werk der französischen ‚Nouvelle vague' machen. (rororo Lexikon des internationalen Films, Reinbek bei Hamburg 1990, Bd. 9, S. 4399/4400)

[23] Alice in den Städten, BRD 1973, Regie: Wim Wenders, Buch: Wim Wenders und Veith von Fürstenberg, 112 Minuten, Uraufführung 17.5.1974

[24] Hohl, Reinhold (Hrsg.): Oskar Schlemmer. Die Fensterbilder, Frankfurt am Main 1988, S. 36. Vgl. auch: Einblicke – Ausblicke. Fensterbilder von der Romantik bis heute, Ausstellungskatalog, Recklinghausen 1976. Vgl. hierzu auch: Paris seen from the window. In: Distel, Anne/Druick, Douglas W. u.a.: Gustave Caillebotte. Urban Impressionist. Ausstellungskatalog Musée d'Orsay, Paris 1995, S. 141-151

[25] Hebbel, Christian Friedrich, Paris ist eine Welt. Briefe und Tagebücher 1843-1844, Herford 1987, S. 93

[26] Proust, Marcel: Auf der Suche nach der verlorenen Zeit (A la recherche du temps perdu, (1913-1927), Frankfurt am Main 1979, S. 2004. Vgl. hierzu auch: Trottenberg, Arthur D. (Hrsg.): Marcel Proust, Eugene Atget. Ein Bild von Paris, Frankfurt am Main 1987, S. 70

[27] Fontane, Theodor: Frau Jenny Treibel. Oder wo sich Herz zu Herzen find't. Roman aus der Berliner Gesellschaft, 1892. Zitiert in: Theodor Fontane: Romane, München 1969, S. 267

[28] George Grosz zitiert in: Riha, Karl: Nachwort zu George Grosz. New York. Op. cit., S. 49

[29] Dreiser, Theodore: The Color of a Great City, 1923, in: Cohen, Barbara/Chwast, Seymour/Heller, Steven (Hrsg.): New York observed. Artists and Writers look at the city, New York 1987, S. 80/81

[30] Lichtenberg, Georg Christoph: Kew Gardens aus: Aphorismen, Essays, Briefe; hrsg. von Kurt Batt, Leipzig 1965, zitiert in: Kohl, Norbert (Hrsg.): London. Eine europäische Metropole in Texten und Bildern, Frankfurt am Main 1979, S. 118

[31] Hebbel, Christian Friedrich: Op. cit., S. 37

[32] Sherwell, Arthur: Life in West London, London 1901

[19] Konrád, György: Die Herausforderung der Großstadt, in: Berner, Peter/Brix, Emil/Mantel, Wolfgang (ed.): Wien um 1900. Aufbruch der Moderne, Vienna 1986, pp. 259–275

[20] Mercier, Louis-Sébastien: op. cit., chapter DL XXXV, p. 82

[21] Rivarol, quoted from Kindlers Literatur Lexikon, vol. 21, Munich 1974, p. 9197

[22] Queneau, Raymond: Zazie dans le métro, Paris 1959; film version: Zazie dans le métro, France 1960, Director: Louis Malle. Script: Louis Malle and Jean Paul Rappenau after a novel by Raymond Queneau, 93 minutes. First screening 20.12.1960. The absurd world of grown-ups, seen through the eyes of a premature child. Little Zazie spends 36 hours discovering Paris; the metropolis shows itself as an urban jungle full of heros, baddies and clowns, full of funny and macabre events. Louis Malle produced this grotesque comedy after a novel by Queneau, attempting a visual translation of the spoken humour throughout. Like the author, who analyses the seeming naivety of the child's language, Malle, too, returns to the childhood days of cinematography: to the slapstick of the Mack-Sennet films and the ancient tricks of Meliès, slow motion, speeding up, repetition and deformation, the abandonment of space and time. Playing with alienation of colour and purposefully false synchronisation are an intellectual corruption of convention, making this film a classical example of the French 'Nouvelle vague'. (rororo Lexikon des internationalen Films, Reinbek near Hamburg 1990, Vol. 9, pp. 4399-4400)

[23] Alice in den Städten, Germany 1973, Director: Wim Wenders, Script: Wim Wenders and Veith von Fürstenberg, 112 minutes, first screening 17.5.1974

[24] Hohl, Reinhold (ed.): Oskar Schlemmer. Die Fensterbilder, Frankfurt am Main 1988, p. 36. Cf. also: Einblicke – Ausblicke. Fensterbilder von der Romantik bis heute, exhibition catalogue, Recklinghausen 1976. Cf. further: Paris seen from the window. In: Distel, Anne/Druick, Douglas W. et al.: Gustave Caillebotte. Urban Impressionist. Exhibition catalogue Musée d'Orsay Paris 1995, pp. 141-151

[25] Hebbel, Christian Friedrich, Paris ist eine Welt. Briefe und Tagebücher 1843-1844, Herford 1987, p. 93

[26] Proust, Marcel: Auf der Suche nach der verlorenen Zeit (A la recherche du temps perdu, (1913-1927), Frankfurt am Main 1979, Cf. also: Trottenberg, Arthur D. (ed.): Marcel Proust, Eugene Atget. A vision of Paris, New York 1963

[27] Fontane, Theodor: Frau Jenny Treibel. Oder wo sich Herz zu Herzen find't. Roman aus der Berliner Gesellschaft, 1892. Citation from: Theodor Fontane: Romane, Munich 1969, p. 267

[28] George Grosz quoted in: Riha, Karl: Epilogue: George Grosz. New York. Op. cit., p. 49

[29] Dreiser, Theodore: The Color of a Great City, 1923, in: Cohen, Barbara/Chwast, Seymour/Heller, Steven (ed.): New York observed. Artists and Writers look at the City, New York 1987, pp. 80-81

[30] Lichtenberg, Georg Christoph: Kew Gardens from: Aphorismen, Essays, Briefe; ed. by Kurt Batt, Leipzig 1965, quoted in: Kohl, Norbert (ed.): London. Eine europäische Metropole in Texten und Bildern, Frankfurt am Main 1979, p. 118

[31] Hebbel, Christian Friedrich: op. cit., p. 37

[32] Sherwell, Arthur: Life in West London, London 1901

[33] Engel, Fritz: Symphonie Berlin, in: Seitz, Robert/Zucker, Heinz (ed.): op. cit., p. 42

[33] Engel, Fritz: Symphonie Berlin, in: Seitz, Robert/Zucker, Heinz (Hrsg.): Op. cit., S. 42

[34] Hebbel, Christian Friedrich: Op. cit., S. 31

[35] Musil, Robert: Der Mann ohne Eigenschaften, 1930, hrsg. von Alfred Frisé, Reinbek bei Hamburg 1978, S. 9

[36] Op. cit., S. 9/10

[37] Döblin, Alfred: Berlin Alexanderplatz. Die Geschichte von Franz Biberkopf, Berlin 1929

[38] Vgl. hierzu: Klotz, Volker: Die erzählte Stadt. Ein Sujet der Herausforderung des Romans von Lesage bis Döblin, München 1969, insbesondere: Die Stadt als Assoziationsfeld, S. 376/377

[39] Mann, Thomas: Der Zauberberg, 2 Bde., Berlin 1924

[40] Johnson, Uwe: Jahrestage. Aus dem Leben von Gesine Cresspahl, 4 Bde., Frankfurt am Main 1970-1983

[41] Vgl. hierzu: Schneider, Peter Paul: Montage-Zeit, in: Schneider, Peter Paul u.a. (Hrsg.): Literatur im Industriezeitalter, Ausstellungskatalog des Deutschen Literaturarchivs im Schiller Nationalmuseum, Marbach am Neckar 1987, S. 731-759

[42] Joyce, James: Ulysses, New York 1918-1920

[43] Dos Passos, John: Manhattan Transfer, Boston 1925

[44] Moholy-Nagy, László: Berlin. Projektionsfotomontage für ein Bühnenbild zu Walter Mehrings „Der Kaufmann von Berlin" Bromsilber, Mattglanz, 25,8 x 38,0 cm, 1929

[45] Tucholsky, Kurt: Deutschland, Deutschland über alles. Ein Bilderbuch von Kurt Tucholsky und vielen Fotografen. Montiert von John Heartfield, Berlin 1929

[46] Berlin. Die Sinfonie der Großstadt, Deutschland 1927, Regie: Walter Ruttmann, Buch: Walter Ruttmann, Karl Freund, 60 Minuten

[47] 42nd Street, USA 1933, Regie: Lloyd Bacon, Ausstattung: Jack Okey, Choreographie: Busby Berkeley, Schauspieler: Ruby Keeler und Dick Powell

[48] Klotz, Volker: Op. cit., S. 372-418

[49] Schneider, Peter-Paul: Um uns die Stadt, in: Schneider, Peter-Paul: Op. cit., S. 693

[50] Miller, Henry: Sexus, Paris 1949, in: Cohen, Barbara u.a. (Hrsg.): Op.cit., S. 69

[51] Metropolis, Deutschland 1926, Regie: Fritz Lang, Drehbuch: Thea von Harbou, Ausstattung: Erich Kettelhut, Otto Hunte, Karl Vollbrecht, Schauspieler: Brigitte Helm, Alfred Abel, 93 Minuten. Vgl. hierzu auch: O.V.: Metropolis un film de Fritz Lang. Images d'un tournage. Une coproduction du centre National de la photographie et de la Cinémathéque Française, Paris1985

[52] Fritz Lang zitiert in: Albrecht, Donald: Architektur im Film. Die Moderne als große Illusion (Designing Dreams. Modern Architecture in the Movies), Berlin 1989, S. 154

[53] Zitiert in: Stephan, Regina (Hrsg.): Erich Mendelsohn. Gebaute Welten, Arbeiten für Europa, Palästina und Amerika, Ausstellungskatalog, Ostfildern Ruit 1998, S. 85

[54] High Treason, USA 1929, Regie: Maurice Alvey, Ausstattung: Andrew L. Mazzei, Schauspieler: Bonita Hume, Jameson Thomas. Just Imagine, USA 1930, Regie: David Buttler, Ausstattung: Stephen Gooson, Schauspieler: Maureen O'Sullivan, El Brendel. Blade Runner, USA 1982, Regie: Ridley Scott, Buch: Hampton Faucher und David People nach einem Roman von Philip K. Dick, 117 Minuten

[34] Hebbel, Christian Friedrich: op. cit., p. 31

[35] Musil, Robert: The Man without Qualities, vol. 1. Translated by Eithne Wilkins and Ernst Kaiser. London 1968, pp. 39 f.

[36] Op. cit., pp. 9-10

[37] Döblin, Alfred: Berlin Alexanderplatz. Die Geschichte von Franz Biberkopf, Berlin 1929

[38] Cf.: Klotz, Volker: Die erzählte Stadt. Ein Sujet der Herausforderung des Romans von Lesage bis Döblin, Munich 1969, particularly: Die Stadt als Assoziationsfeld, pp. 376-377

[39] Mann, Thomas: Der Zauberberg (The Magic Mountain), 2 vols., Berlin 1924

[40] Johnson, Uwe: Jahrestage. Aus dem Leben von Gesine Cresspahl, 4 vols., Frankfurt am Main 1970-1983

[41] Cf.: Schneider, Peter Paul: Montage-Zeit, in: Schneider, Peter Paul et al. (ed.): Literatur im Industriezeitalter, Exhibition catalogue of Deutsches Literaturarchiv in the Schiller Nationalmuseum, Marbach am Neckar 1987, pp. 731-759

[42] Joyce, James: Ulysses, New York 1918-1920

[43] Dos Passos, John: Manhattan Transfer, Boston 1925

[44] Moholy-Nagy, László: Berlin. Projection photomontage for a stage set for Walter Mehrings "Der Kaufmann von Berlin" silver bromide, matt finish, 25.8 x 38.0 cm, 1929

[45] Tucholsky, Kurt: Deutschland, Deutschland über alles. A picture book by Kurt Tucholsky and many photographers. Assembled by John Heartfield, Berlin 1929

[46] Berlin. Die Sinfonie der Großstadt, Deutschland 1927, Director: Walter Ruttmann, Script: Walter Ruttmann, Karl Freund, 60 minutes.

[47] 42nd Street, USA 1933, Director: Lloyd Bacon, Sets and Costumes: Jack Okey, Choreography: Busby Berkeley, Actors: Ruby Keeler and Dick Powell

[48] Klotz, Volker: op. cit., pp. 372-418

[49] Schneider, Peter-Paul: Um uns die Stadt, in: Schneider, Peter-Paul: op. cit., p. 693

[50] Miller, Henry: Sexus, Paris 1949, in: Cohen, Barbara et al. (ed.): op.cit., p. 69

[51] Metropolis, Deutschland 1926, Director: Fritz Lang, Script: Thea von Harbou, Sets and Costumes: Erich Kettelhut, Otto Hunte, Karl Vollbrecht, Actors: Brigitte Helm, Alfred Abel, 93 minutes. Cf. also: N.N.: Metropolis un film de Fritz Lang. Images d'un tournage. Une coproduction du centre National de la photographie et de la Cinémathéque Française, Paris 1985

[52] Fritz Lang quoted in: Albrecht, Donald: Architektur im Film. Die Moderne als große Illusion (Designing Dreams. Modern Architecture in the Movies), Berlin 1989, p. 154

[53] Quoted in: Stephan, Regina (ed.): Erich Mendelsohn. Gebaute Welten, Arbeiten für Europa, Palästina und Amerika, Ausstellungskatalog, Ostfildern Ruit 1998, p. 85

[54] High Treason, USA 1929, Director: Maurice Alvey, Sets and Costumes: Andrew L. Mazzei, Actors: Bonita Hume, Jameson Thomas. Just Imagine, USA 1930, Director: David Buttler, Sets and Costumes: Stephen Gooson, Actors: Maureen O'Sullivan, El Brendel. Blade Runner, USA 1982, Director: Ridley Scott, Script: Hampton Faucher and David People after a novel by Philip K. Dick, 117 minutes.

[55] Zu Moses King und Hugh Ferriss vgl.: „Kings Views. New York," Moses King 1909; „King's Views of New York", New York, Moses King 1911, 1919, 1922 und 1926. Zeichnungen von u.a.: Harry M. Pettit und Richard W. Rummel; Ferriss, Hugh: The Metropolis of Tomorrow, New York 1929, Neuauflage, New York 1986. Vgl. hierzu auch: Ferriss Leich, Jean: Architectural Visions. The Drawings of Hugh Ferriss, New York 1980

[56] Sue, Eugène: Les mystères de Paris, Paris 1842/43 (Die Geheimnisse von Paris), 8 Bde., Berlin 1843

[57] Riis, Jacob, A.: How the other half lives, New York 1890, Neuauflage New York 1971. Vgl. hierzu: Jackson, Gregory S.: Cultivating Spiritual Sight: Jacob Riis's Virtual-Tour Narrative and the Visual Modernization of Protestant Homiletics. In: representations 83, University of California, Berkeley 2003

[58] Hugo, Victor: Die Elenden, Zürich 1993, S. 109. Erstausgabe: Les miserables, Paris 1862

[59] Der verlorene Sohn, Deutschland 1934, Regie: Luis Trenker; Produktion: Ufa, Drehbuch: Luis Trenker, Arnold Ulitz, Reinhart Steinbicker, Kamera: Albert Benitz, Reimar Kuntze, Schauspieler: Luis Trenker, Maria Andergast, Bertl Schultes, Marian Marsh, Eduard Köck, 80 Minuten

[60] Nietzsche, Friedrich: Also sprach Zarathustra, Leipzig 1883/84 (1.-3. Teil), Leipzig 1885 (4. Teil), Stuttgart 1980, S. 165

[61] Rilke, Rainer Maria: Stundenbuch, 1905, zitiert in: Riha, Karl: Deutsche Großstadtlyrik, Zürich 1983, S. 59

[62] Spengler, Oswald: Der Untergang des Abendlandes. Umrisse zu einer Morphologie der Weltgeschichte; Bd. 1: Gestalt u. Wirklichkeit, Wien 1918; Bd. 2: Welthistorische Perspektiven, München 1922

[63] Op. cit., Ausgabe München 1963, S. 673

[64] Ibidem, S. 676.

[65] Thoreau, Henry David: Letter to R.W. Emerson, in: The Writings of Henry David Thoreau. Familiar Letters. Years of Discipline, Boston 1894. In: Cohen, Barbara/ Chwast, Seymour/Heller, Steven (Hrsg.): New York Observed. Artists and Writers Look at the City, New York 1987, S. 99

[66] Sandburg, Carl: Chicago, in: Sandburg, Carl: Guten Morgen, Amerika. Ausgewählte Gedichte, Berlin 1948, zitiert in: Schneider, Peter-Paul u.a. (Hrsg.): Op. cit., S. 455

[67] Dreiser, Theodore: My City, 1929, in: Cohen, Barbara u.a. (Hrsg.): Op. cit., S. 113

[68] Simmel, Georg: Die Großstädte und das Geistesleben, in: Die Großstadt, Dresden 1903

[69] Op. cit., S. 188f.

[70] Roters, Eberhard: Die Straße, in: Roters, Eberhard/Schulz, Bernhard (Hrsg.): Ich und die Stadt. Mensch und Großstadt in der deutschen Kunst des 20. Jahrhunderts. Ausstellungskatalog Berlinische Galerie, Berlin 1987, S. 35-58

[71] Wenders, Wim; Op. cit., S. 139

[72] Hebbel, Christian Friedrich: Op. cit., S. 50/51

[73] Op. cit., S. 54

[74] Op. cit., S. 13

[75] Chagall, Marc: Bonjour Paris. 23 Lithographien mit einer Einführung von Wolf Stadler, Freiburg im Breisgau 1983, S. 16. Chagall konnte 1910 als dreiundzwanzigjähriger Stipendiat das erste Mal nach Paris reisen.

[55] For Moses King and Hugh Ferris cf.: "Kings Views. New York", Moses King 1909; "King's Views of New York", New York, Moses King 1911, 1919, 1922 and 1926. Drawings by: Harry M. Pettit and Richard W. Rummel et al.; Ferris, Hugh: The Metropolis of Tomorrow, New York 1929, new edition New York 1986. Cf. also: Ferris Leich, Jean: Architectural Visions. The Drawings of Hugh Ferris, New York 1980

[56] Sue, Eugène: Les mystères de Paris, Paris 1842/43 (The Mysteries of Paris), 8 vols., Berlin 1843

[57] Riis, Jacob, A.: How the other half lives, New York 1890, new edition New York 1971. Cf.: Jackson, Gregory S.: Cultivating Spiritual Sight: Jacob Riis's Virtual-Tour Narrative and the visual Modernization of Protestant Homiletics. In: representations 83, University of California, Berkeley 2003

[58] Hugo, Victor: Les Misèrables. English translation by Isabel Florence Hapgood, London 1903, p. 106

[59] Der verlorene Sohn, Deutschland 1934, Director: Luis Trenker; Producer: Ufa, Script: Luis Trenker, Arnold Ulitz, Reinhart Steinbicker, Camera: Albert Benitz, Reimar Kuntze, Actors: Luis Trenker, Maria Andergast, Bertl Schultes, Marian Marsh, Eduard Köck, 80 minutes

[60] Nietzsche, Friedrich: Also sprach Zarathustra, Leipzig 1883/84 (Parts 1-3), Leipzig 1885 (Part 4), Stuttgart 1980, p. 165

[61] Rilke, Rainer Maria: Stundenbuch, 1905, quoted in: Riha, Karl: Deutsche Großstadtlyrik, Zürich 1983, p. 59

[62] Spengler, Oswald: Der Untergang des Abendlandes. Umrisse zu einer Morphologie der Weltgeschichte; Vol. 1: Gestalt u. Wirklichkeit, Vienna 1918; vol. 2: Welthistorische Perspektiven, Munich 1922

[63] Op. cit., edition Munich 1963, p. 673

[64] Ibidem, p. 676.

[65] Thoreau, Henry David: Letter to R.W. Emerson, in: The Writings of Henry David Thoreau. Familiar Letters. Years of Discipline, Boston 1894. In: Cohen, Barbara/Chwast, Seymour/Heller, Steven (ed.): New York Observed. Artists and Writers Look at the City, New York 1987, p. 99

[66] Sandburg, Carl: Chicago, in: Sandburg, Carl: Guten Morgen, Amerika. Ausgewählte Gedichte, Berlin 1948, quoted in: Schneider, Peter-Paul et al. (ed.): op. cit., p. 455

[67] Dreiser, Theodore: My City, 1929, in: Cohen, Barbara et al. (ed.): op. cit., p. 113

[68] Simmel, Georg: Die Großstädte und das Geistesleben, in: Die Großstadt, Dresden 1903

[69] Op. cit., pp. 188 f.

[70] Roters, Eberhard: Die Straße, in: Roters, Eberhard/Schulz, Bernhard (ed.): Ich und die Stadt. Mensch und Großstadt in der deutschen Kunst des 20. Jahrhunderts, exhibition catalogue Berlinische Galerie, Berlin 1987, pp. 35-58

[71] Wenders, Wim: op. cit., p. 139

[72] Hebbel, Christian Friedrich: op. cit., pp. 50-51

[73] Op. cit., p. 54

[74] Op. cit., p. 113

[75] Chagall, Marc: Bonjour Paris. 23 Lithographs with an introduction by Wolf Stadler, Freiburg im Breisgau 1983, p. 16
Chagall was awarded a scholarship at the age of 23 and travelled to Paris for the first time in 1910.

[76] Cendrars, Blaise and Fernand Léger: Paris. Ma ville, Paris 1987, p. 7

[77] Rilke, Rainer Maria: Die Aufzeichnungen des Malte Laurids Brigge, Leipzig 1910. Novel in the form of a diary, started in 1904 in Rome under the influence of the impressions of his first stay in Paris 1902/03, finished in 1908 to 1910 in Paris.

[76] Cendrars, Blaise und Fernand Léger: Paris. Ma ville, Paris 1987, S. 7

[77] Rilke, Rainer Maria: Die Aufzeichnungen des Malte Laurids Brigge, Leipzig 1910. Tagebuchroman, begonnen 1904 in Rom unter dem Eindruck des ersten Parisaufenthaltes 1902/1903, vollendet 1908 bis 1910 in Paris

[78] Rilke, Rainer Maria: Brief vom 10. August 1915 an Erica Hauptmann in München. Zitiert in: Schneider, Paul u.a.: Literatur im Industriezeitalter. Ausstellungskatalog des Deutschen Literaturarchivs im Schiller Nationalmuseum, Marbach am Neckar 1987, S. 707

[79] Rilke, Rainer Maria: Brief an Helene von Nostiz Berlin, vom 8. Februar 1910. In: Rainer Maria Rilke Helene von Nostiz. Briefwechsel. Frankfurt/M. 1976, S. 19f

[80] Le Corbusier: Brief an die Eltern am 21. Juni aus Naumburg und Weimar. In: Gresleri, Giuliano: Le Corbusier. Reise nach dem Orient. Unveröffentlichte Briefe und zum Teil noch nicht publizierte Texte und Photographien von Eduard Jeanneret. Mit einigen Bemerkungen von Italo Zannier über den Photographen Jeanneret. Zürich 1991 (Paris 1984), S. 401/402

[81] Steinbeck, John: Autobiography. The Making of a New Yorker, 1953, in: Cohen, Barbara u.a. (Hrsg.): Op. cit., S. 122

[82] George Grosz zitiert in: Riha, Karl: Nachwort zu: George Grosz. New York: Op. cit., S. 48

[83] Dreiser, Theodore: My City, 1929, in: Cohen, Barbara u.a. (Hrsg.): Op. cit., S. 113

[84] Wolfe, Thomas: The Web and the Rock, 1939, in: Cohen, Barbara u.a. (Hrsg.): Op. cit., S. 19

[78] Rilke, Rainer Maria: Letter dated 10th August 1915 to Erica Hauptmann in Munich. Citation from: Schneider, Paul et al.: Literatur im Industriezeitalter. Exhibition catalogue of Deutsches Literaturarchivs in the Schiller Nationalmuseum, Marbach am Neckar 1987, p. 707

[79] Rilke, Rainer Maria: Letter to Helene von Nostiz in Berlin, February 8th, 1910. In: Rainer Maria Rilke Helene von Nostiz. Briefwechsel. Frankfurt/M. 1976, pp. 19f

[80] Le Corbusier: Letter to his parents dated June 21st from Naumburg and Weimar. In: Gresleri, Giuliano: Le Corbusier. Reise nach dem Orient. Unveröffentlichte Briefe und zum Teil noch nicht publizierte Texte und Photographien von Eduard Jeanneret. Mit einigen Bemerkungen von Italo Zannier über den Photographen Jeanneret. Zurich 1991 (Paris 1984), p. 401/402

[81] Steinbeck, John: Autobiography. The Making of a New Yorker, 1953, in: Cohen, Barbara et al. (ed.): op. cit., p. 122

[82] George Grosz quoted in: Riha, Karl: Epilogue for: George Grosz. New York: op. cit., p. 48

[83] Dreiser, Theodore: My City, 1929, in: Cohen, Barbara et al. (ed.): op. cit., p. 113

[83] Wolfe, Thomas: The Web and the Rock, 1939, in: Cohen, Barbara et al. (ed.): op. cit., p. 19

Anmerkungen „Europäische Metropolen im Wandel“

[1] Häußermann, Hartmut und Walter Siebel: Neue Urbanität, Franfurt am Main 1987, S. 239.

[2] Berlin. Die Sinfonie der Großstadt, Deutschland 1927, Regie: Walter Ruttmann, Buch: Walter Ruttmann, Karl Freund, 60 Minuten.

[3] Thot, Jennifer: The Mole People. Life in the Tunnels Beneath New York City, Chicago 1994. Deutsche Ausgabe: Das Leben unter New York City, Berlin 1994.

[4] Die Literatur zu diesen Thema wächst je mehr die Stadt zu einer Ware degradiert, eine Entwicklung die mit der Kapitalisierung des Bodens begann. Die Vielzahl der Publikationen ist Oberflächenvermarktungsliteratur. Doch es gibt auch Ausnahmen, Bücher, in denen sich die Autoren nicht nur mit dem Verkaufen der Stadt, sondern auch mit dem Wesen, dem Sein derselben auseinandersetzen wie z.B.: Hilber, Maria Luise und Ayda Ergez: Stadtidentität. Der richtige Weg zum Stadtmarketing, Zürich 2004 und Müller, Michael und Franz Dröge: Die ausgestellte Stadt. Zur Differenz von Ort und Raum. Basel, Boston und Berlin 2005.

[5] Whyte, William Holy: The Social Life of Small Urban Spaces, Washington D.C. 1980. Und: Tate, Allan: Great City Parks, London 2001, S. 4-9. Sowie: Dutli, Peter, Jörg Esefeld und Pierre Kreis: Neue Stadträume in Barcelona. Stadterneuerung durch Plätze, Parkanlagen, Straßenräume und Skulpturen, Zürich 1991.

[6] Bollerey, Franziska: Martin Wagners „Politopolis“ oder Berlin die Metropole für alle. In: Schwarz, Karl (Hrsg.): Die Zukunft der Metropolen. Paris, London, New York, Berlin, 1984, S. 365-376.

[7] Kraus, Karl: Die letzten Tage der Menschheit. Tragödie in fünf Akten mit Vorspiel und Epilog. (1918/19), Wien 1922. Zitiert in ders.: Auswahl aus dem Werk, München 1976, S. 48.

[8] Musil, Robert: Der Mann ohne Eigenschaften, Reinbek bei Hamburg 1981, S. 16.

Notes "The Changing Face of the European Metropolis"

[1] Häußermann, Hartmut/Siebel, Walter: Neue Urbanität, Frankfurt a.M. 1987, p. 239

[2] Berlin. Die Sinfonie der Großstadt, Germany 1927, Director: Walter Ruttmann; Book: Walter Ruttmann/Karl Freund, 60 minutes

[3] Toth, Jennifer: The Mole People. Life in the tunnels beneath New York City, Chicago 1993

[4] There is a growing number of publications discussing the purchasable character of the city, a tendency which arose with the capitalization of the soil. Above all, these books discuss marketing strategies, with some exceptions, where urban culture is discussed, as for example: Hilber, Maria Luise and Ayda Ergez: Stadtidentität. Der richtige Weg zum Stadtmarketing, Zürich 2004 and Müller, Michael and Franz Dröge: Die ausgestellte Stadt. Zur Differenz von Ort und Raum. Basel, Boston and Berlin 2005.

[5] Whyte, William Holy: The Social Life of Small Urban Spaces, Washington D.C. 1980. As well as: Dutli, Peter/Esefeld, Jörg/Kreis, Pierre: Neue Stadträume in Barcelona. Stadterneuerung durch Plätze, Parkanlagen, Straßenräume und Skulpturen, Zurich 1991

[6] Bollerey, Franziska: Martin Wagners "Politopolis" oder Berlin die Metropole für alle. In: Karl Schwarz (ed.): Die Zukunft der Metropolen, Paris/London/New York/Berlin, Berlin1984, pp. 365-376

[7] Kraus, Karl: Die letzten Tage der Menschheit. Tragödie in fünf Akten mit Vorspiel und Epilog (1918/19), Wien 1922. Cited after: Karl Kraus: Auswahl aus dem Werk, Munich 1957, p. 48

[8] Musil, Robert: Der Mann ohne Eigenschaften, Reinbek bei Hamburg 1981, p. 16

Abbildungsverzeichnis

List of Illustrations

25 Brandmauern in der Lindenstraße, Berlin-Kreuzberg, um 1980, Fotografie Franziska Bollerey

26 Brandmauern in der Lindenstraße, Berlin-Kreuzberg, um 1980, Fotografie Franziska Bollerey

27 Hinterhöfe in der Lehrter Straße, Berlin-Moabit, Fotografie Franziska Bollerey, Juni 1983

28 Alfred Pfitzner, Berliner Hinterhäuser im Winter. Blick in den Hinterhof des ehemaligen Künstlerhauses in der Bellevuestraße, Berlin Tiergarten. Öl auf Leinwand (75 x 84,5 cm) 1930. Berlin, Stiftung Stadtmuseum. Inv. Nr. GEM 69/15. Hier bin ich der Kuratorin Frau Dr. Angelika Reimer zu Dank verpflichtet.

29 Brandmauer in der Groninger Straße, Berlin-Wedding, Fotografie Franziska Bollerey, Juli 1987, Plan Nr. 9

30 Brandmauer in der Düsseldorfer Straße, Berlin-Wilmersdorf, Fotografie Franziska Bollerey, 1980er Jahre

31 Plan Monumental von Berlin, Carl Glück Verlag, Farbdruck (37 x 49,6 cm), 1860. In: Spitzer, Heinz/Zimm, Alfred: Berlin von 1650 bis 1900. Entwicklung der Stadt in historischen Plänen mit Erläuterungen. Berlin 1989 [1987], Plan Nr. 9

32 H. Guesnu, Plan simplifié, indispensable aux étrangers pour se guider seul dans Paris, Excursion dans Paris sans voitures. Nouveau guide du promeneur, um 1867. In: Cameron, Robert/Salinger, Pierre: Above Paris, San Francisco 1985, S. 26

33 Johannes Grützke, Berlin, Ein „erleuchteter" Mann öffnet seinen Morgenrock und Brandenburger Tor und Funkturm quellen hervor (Angaben aus dem Werkbuch von Johannes Grützke). Gouache, Pastell auf Leimfarbe auf zwei zusammengeleimten Packpapieren (130x 100 cm), 1985. Stiftung Stadtmuseum Berlin. Hier bin ich Frau Karoline Müller, Ladengalerie Brunnenstraße 5 zu Dank verpflichtet.

34 Gilbert Legrand, Vergeßt Paris nicht, Öl auf Leinwand. In: Köhler, Michael: Der Eiffelturm. Geschichten, Kuriositäten und Fakten um den berühmtesten Turm der Welt, München 1990, S. 116

35 Abrißwand im Quartier Goutte d'Or, Paris, Fotografie Franziska Bollerey, April 1990

36 George Grosz, Die Großstadt, Öl auf Leinwand (100 x 102 cm), Lugano, Sammlung Thyssen Bornemisza, 1916/1917. In: Stadtbilder. Berlin in der Malerei vom 17. Jahrhundert bis zur Gegenwart. Ausstellungskatalog Berlin Museum, Berlin 1987, S. 270-272

37 Christa Dichgans, N.Y. Memories, (200 x 160 cm), 1981 ausgestellt im Göttinger Kunstverein. In: „Zeitmagazin", 34/1981

38 Lichtreklame, Tokio, 1994

39 Plastiktüte ‚Elbeo', 1980

40 Plastiktüte ‚New Yorker', Chur 1991

41 Nikolaus Braun, Berliner Straßenszene, Öl auf Hartfaser (74 x 103 cm), 1921. In: Roters, Eberhard/Stock, Wolfgang Jean: Weltstadtsinfonie. Berliner Realismus 1900-1950, Ausstellungskatalog Kunstverein München 1984, S. 41 und 126

42 Giovanni Battista Piranesi: Idea delle antiche Vie Appia e Ardeatina (Idealansicht der antiken Straßen Appia und Ardeatina). Radierung (52,9 x 41cm). Frontispiz Bd. 2 der „Antichita Romane", 4 Bände, Rom 1784; erstmals in „Lettere di Giustificazione", 1757. In: Höper, Corinna (Hrsg.): Giovanni Battista Piranesi. Die poetische Wahrheit. Ausstellungskatalog Staatsgalerie Stuttgart, 1999, S. 114, Abb. 30

24 Henry Ries, Children playing in front of a destroyed building which serves as a home (Berlin), 1948, Berlin, Landesarchiv, photo no. 160968. In: Ries, Henry: Ich war ein Berliner. Erinnerungen eines New Yorker Fotojournalisten, Berlin 2001, S. 79. Caption in the book: Das Leben geht weiter (life goes on)

25 Fire Walls in Lindenstraße, Berlin-Kreuzberg, photograph Franziska Bollerey, around 1980

26 Fire Walls in Lindenstraße, Berlin-Kreuzberg, photograph Franziska Bollerey, around 1980

27 Back Yards in Lehrter Straße, Berlin-Moabit, photograph Franziska Bollerey, June 1983

28 Alfred Pfitzner, Berliner Hinterhäuser im Winter. Blick in den Hinterhof des ehemaligen Künstlerhauses in der Bellevuestraße (backyard of the former artist's house in Bellevuestraße in Berlin Tiergarten). Oil on canvas (75 x 84,5 cm), 1930. Berlin, Stiftung Stadtmuseum. Inv. No. GEM 69/15. Here I owe thanks to the curator, Dr. Angelika Reimer.

29 Fire Wall in Groninger Straße, Berlin-Wedding, photograph Franziska Bollerey, July 1987

30 Fire Wall in Düsseldorfer Straße, Berlin-Wilmersdorf, photograph Franziska Bollerey, 1980ies

31 Monumental Map of Berlin, Carl Glück Verlag, colour print (37 x 49.6 cm), 1860. In: Spitzer, Heinz/Zimm, Alfred: Berlin von 1650 bis 1900. Entwicklung der Stadt in historischen Plänen mit Erläuterungen. Berlin 1989 [1987], map no. 9

32 H. Guesnu, Plan simplifié, indispensable aux étrangers pour se guider seul dans Paris, Excursion dans Paris sans voitures. Nouveau guide du promeneur, around 1867. In: Cameron, Robert/Salinger, Pierre: Above Paris, San Francisco 1985, S. 26

33 Johannes Grützke, Berlin, "lighted-up" man opening his gown with the Brandenburg gate and the radiotower bursting from his breast (Note in the scrapbook of Johannes Grützke). Gouache, pastel on lime-water-colour on limed packing paper (130 x 100 cm) With acknowledgement to Karoline Müller, Ladengalerie Brunnenstraße 5, Berlin.

34 Gilbert Legrand, Don't Forget Paris, oil on canvas. In: Köhler, Michael: Der Eiffelturm. Geschichten, Kuriositäten und Fakten um den berühmtesten Turm der Welt, Munich 1990, p. 116

35 Wall of a Demolished Building in the Quartier Goutte d'Or, Paris, photograph Franziska Bollerey, April 1990

36 George Grosz, Die Großstadt (The Metropolis), oil on canvas (100 x 102 cm), Lugano, Thyssen Bornemisza Collection, 1916/1917. In: Stadtbilder. Berlin in der Malerei vom 17. Jahrhundert bis zur Gegenwart. Exhibition catalogue Berlin Museum, Berlin 1987, pp. 270-272

37 Christa Dichgans, N.Y. Memories, (200 x 160 cm), 1981 exhibited in the gallery of Göttinger Kunstverein. In: "Zeitmagazin" 34/1981

38 Neon advertisements, Tokyo, 1994

39 Plastic bag 'Elbeo', 1980

40 Plastic bag 'New Yorker', Chur 1991

41 Nikolaus Braun, Berliner Straßenszene (Street Szene in Berlin), oil on hardboard (74 x 103 cm), 1921. In: Roters, Eberhard/Stock, Wolfgang Jean: Weltstadtsinfonie. Berliner Realismus 1900-1950, exhibition catalogue Kunstverein Munich 1984, p. 41 and p. 126

43 Giovanni Battista Piranesi: Pianta di Roma (Plan von Rom). Radierung (54,1 x 76,9 cm). „Pianta di Roma disegnata colla situazione di tutti Monumenti antichi, de' quali in oggi ancora se ne vedono gli avanzi, ed/illustrata colli Frammenti di Marmo della Pianta di Roma antica, scavati, saranno due secoli, nelle Rovine del Tempio di Romolo; ed ora esistenti nel Museo di Campidoglio", 1784 (1756). In: Höper, Corinna (Hrsg.): Giovanni Battista Piranesi. Die poetische Wahrheit. Ausstellungskatalog Staatsgalerie Stuttgart, 1999, S. 168, Abb. 108

44 Porträt von Louis-Sébastien Mercier, Stahlstich von Torchiana nach einer Zeichnung von Sergent Marceau. In: Bourguinat, Elisabeth: Les rues de Paris au XVIII siècle, Ausstellungskatalog Musée Carnavalet Paris 1999, S. 6

45 A beau cacher, gut verborgen. Kupferstich von L.M. Bonnet, 1772. In: Bourguinat, Elisabeth: Les rues de Paris au XVIII siècle, Ausstellungskatalog Musée Carnavalet Paris 1999, S. 23

46 Umschlag zu Raymond Queneau, Zazie dans le métro, Taschenbuchausgabe, Verlag Gallimard, Paris 1959

47 Jacob Steinhardt, Die Stadt, Öl auf Leinwand (61 x 40 cm), 1913, Berlin, Staatliche Museen Preußischer Kulturbesitz, Nationalgalerie. In: Stadtbilder. Berlin in der Malerei vom 17. Jahrhundert bis zur Gegenwart, Ausstellungskatalog Berlin Museum, Berlin 1987, S. 293/294

48 Fernand Léger, Blick aus dem Fenster, Lithographie. In: Fernand Léger/Blaise Cendrars, Paris. Ma Ville, (1954-1957), Bibliothèque des Arts, Paris 1987 und München 1987, S. 71

49 Oskar Schlemmer, Wohnraum mit arbeitender Frau, Öl über Bleistift und Farbstift auf kaschiertem Karton (32,3 x 19,8 cm), 1942, Basel, Kunstmuseum. In: Hohl, Reinhold (Hrsg.): Oskar Schlemmer. Die Fensterbilder, Frankfurt/Main 1988, Tafel 6

50 Oskar Schlemmer, Am Fenster, Öl über Bleistift auf kaschiertem Karton (31 x 22,6 cm), 1942, Wuppertal, Von der Heydt-Museum. In: Hohl, Reinhold (Hrsg.): Oskar Schlemmer. Die Fensterbilder, Frankfurt/Main 1988, Tafel 11

51 Gisèle Freund, Jean Paul Sartre schaut auf St. Germain-des-Près, Fotografie, 1959. In: Caujolle, Christian: Gisèle Freund. Photographien, München 1985, S. 138, Abb. 130

52 Gustave Caillebotte, Homme au balcon, auch als homme au balcon, Boulevard Haussmann bekannt, Öl auf Leinwand (117 x 90 cm), 1880, Privatbesitz. In: Distel, Anne/Druick, Douglas W.: Gustave Caillebotte. Urban Impressionist, Ausstellungskatalog Musée d'Orsay Paris 1995, S. 169

53 Edward Hopper, New York Office, Öl auf Leinwand (101,6 x 139,7 cm), 1962, The Kennedy Galleries, New York City. In: Chwast, Seymour/Heller, Steven: The Art of New York, New York 1983, S. 110-111

54 Edward Hopper, Room in Brooklyn, Öl auf Leinwand (76,2 x 86,4 cm), Boston, Museum of Fine Arts, 1932. In: Chwast, Seymour/Heller, Steven: The Art of New York, New York 1983, S. 113

55 George Bellows, Riverfront No. 1 (Coney Island), Öl auf Leinwand (115,3 x 236,7 cm), Columbus (Ohio), Columbus Museum of Art, 1915. In: Chwast, Seymour/Heller, Steven: The Art of New York, New York 1983, S. 62-63

56 George Grosz, Schuhputzer, Zeichnung, 1932. In: George Grosz: New York, hrsg. von Walter Huder und Karl Riha, Siegen 1985

57 Miguel Covarrubias, Harlem, Aquarellzeichnung, 1934. In: Cohen, Barbara/ Chwast, Seymour/Heller, Steven: New York Observed. Artists and Writers look at the City, New York 1987, S. 91

42 Giovanni Battista Piranesi: Idea delle antiche Vie Appia e Ardeatina (ideal vision of the classical streets Appia and Ardeatina). Etching (52,9 x 41cm). Frontispiece of volume 2 of "Antichita Romane", 4 volumes, Rome 1784; first published in "Lettere di Giustificazione", 1757. In: Höper, Corinna (ed.): Giovanni Battista Piranesi. Die poetische Wahrheit. Exhibition catalogue Staatsgalerie Stuttgart, 1999, p. 114, illus. 30

43 Giovanni Battista Piranesi, Pianta di Roma, (map of Rome). Etching (54,1 x 76,9cm) "Pianta di Roma disegnata colla situazione di tutti Monumenti antichi, de' quali in oggi ancora se ne vedono gli avanzi, ed/illustrata colli Frammenti di Marmo della Pianta di Roma antica, scavati, saranno due secoli, nelle Rovine del Tempio di Romolo; ed ora esistenti nel Museo di Campidoglio", 1784 (1756). In: Höper, Corinna (ed.): Giovanni Battista Piranesi. Die poetische Wahrheit. Exhibition catalogue Staatsgalerie Stuttgart, 1999, S. 168, illus. 108

44 Portrait of Louis-Sébastien Mercier, steel engraving by Torchiana after a drawing by Sergent Marceau. In: Bourguinat, Elisabeth: Les rues de Paris au XVIII siècle, exhibition catalogue Musée Carnavalet, Paris 1999, p. 168, illus. 108

45 A beau cacher, (Well Concealed). Engraving by L.M. Bonnet, 1772. In: cf. 44, p. 23

46 Cover for Raymond Queneau, Zazie dans le métro, paper back edition, Gallimard, Paris 1959

47 Jacob Steinhardt, Die Stadt (The City), oil on canvas (61 x 40 cm), 1913, Berlin, Staatliche Museen Preußischer Kulturbesitz, Nationalgalerie. In: Stadtbilder. Berlin in der Malerei vom 17. Jahrhundert bis zur Gegenwart, exhibition catalogue Berlin Museum, Berlin 1987, p. 293/294

48 Fernand Léger, Blick aus dem Fenster, lithograph. In: Fernand Léger/Blaise Cendrars, Paris. Ma Ville, (1954-1957), Bibliothèque des Arts, Paris 1987 and München 1987, S. 71

49 Oskar Schlemmer, Am Fenster, oil over pencil on lined cardboard (31 x 22.6 cm), 1942, Wuppertal, Von der Heydt-Museum. In: Hohl, Reinhold (ed.): Oskar Schlemmer. Die Fensterbilder, Frankfurt/Main 1988, pl. 11

50 Oskar Schlemmer, Wohnraum mit arbeitender Frau (Living Room with Working Woman), oil over pencil and coloured pencil on lined cardboard (32.3 x 19.8 cm), 1942, Basel, Kunstmuseum. In: Hohl, Reinhold (ed.): Oskar Schlemmer. Die Fensterbilder, Frankfurt/Main 1988, pl. 6

51 Gisèle Freund, Jean Paul Sartre looking at St. Germain-des-Près, photograph, 1959. In: Caujolle, Christian: Gisèle Freund. Photographien, Munich 1985, p. 138, fig. 130

52 Gustave Caillebotte, Homme au balcon; also known as: homme au balcon, Boulevard Haussmann (Young Man at a Window), oil on canvas (117 x 90 cm), 1880, private collection. In: Distel, Anne/ Druick, Douglas W.: Gustave Caillebotte. Urban Impressionist, exhibition catalogue Musée d'Orsay, Paris 1995, p. 169

53 Edward Hopper, New York Office, oil on canvas (101,6 x 139,7 cm), 1962, The Kennedy Galleries, New York City. In: Chwast, Seymour/Heller, Steven: The Art of New York, New York 1983, pp. 110-111

54 Edward Hopper, Room in Brooklyn, oil on canvas (76,2 x 86,4 cm), Boston, Museum of Fine Arts, 1932. In: Chwast, Seymour/Heller, Steven: The Art of New York, New York 1983, p. 113

58 Mott Street China Town, New York, Fotografie, 1898

59 Umberto Boccioni, Rissa in Galleria, Öl auf Leinwand (76 x 64 cm), 1910, Mailand, Pinacoteca di Brera. In: Schneede, Uwe M.: Umberto Boccioni, Stuttgart 1994, S. 56 und 210

60 Berenice Abbott, Herald Square, Manhattan, Fotografie, 16. Juli 1936. In: Lloyd, Valérie: New York in the Thirties. The photographs of Berenice Abbott, Side Gallery, Newcastle-upon-Tyne 1977, Kat.-Nr. 59

61 Gustave Doré, A City Thoroughfare, Holzstich, 1872. In: Gustave Doré/Blanchard Jerrold: London. A Pilgrimage, London 1872, nach S. 182

62 Gustave Doré, Ludgate Hill, Holzstich, 1872. In: Gustave Doré/Blanchard Jerrold: London. A Pilgrimage, London 1872, nach S. 48

63 Werner Heldt, Berlin am Meer, Öl auf Leinwand (48 x 84 cm), Privatbesitz, 1952. In: Roters, Eberhard/Schulz, Bernhard: Ich und die Stadt. Mensch und Großstadt in der deutschen Kunst des 20. Jahrhunderts, Ausstellungskatalog Berlinische Galerie, Berlin 1987, S. 344-345

64 Craig McPherson, Autumn, Öl auf Leinwand, 1980, New York, Museum of the City of New York. In: Chwast, Seymour/Heller, Steven: The Art of New York, New York 1983, S. 48/49

65 Montmartre, Sonnenuntergang, Fotografie Franziska Bollerey, April 1990

66 Lichtreklame Bond Clothing Store, New York City, 1948-1954. Acacia Card Co., um 1950. In: Tucker, Kerry: Greetings from New York. A visit to Manhattan in Postcards, New York 1981, S. 72

67 Nächtlich beleuchteter Dachgarten des Hotels Astor am Broadway New York City. Malcolm & Hays, um 1908. In: Tucker, Kerry: Greetings from New York. A visit to Manhattan in Postcards, New York 1981, S. 74

68 Cor van Eesteren, Straßenkreuzung in Paris, Fotografie, um 1925, Archiv N.A.I. Rotterdam

69 Richard Matz, Weltstadtverkehr (Berlin-Alexanderplatz), Farblithographie (67,9 x 95,9 cm), um 1933, Berlin, Privatbesitz. In: Korff, Gottfried/Rürup, Reinhard: Berlin, Berlin. Die Ausstellung zur Geschichte der Stadt, Ausstellungskatalog, Berlin 1987, S. 475

70 Paul Citroën, Metropolis, Collage aus Zeitungsausschnitten und Teilen von Bildpostkarten (76,1 x 58,4 cm), 1923, Faksimile, Fotoarchiv der Rijksuniversiteit Leiden. In: Dethier, Jean (Hrsg.): La ville, art et architecture en Europe, 1870-1933, Ausstellungskatalog Centre Pompidou Paris 1994, S. 258

71 El Lissitzky, The runners, Photomontage (12 x 21,4 cm), 1930, Privatbesitz, Galerie Berinson, Berlin. In: El Lissitzky: 1890-1941. Architect, Painter, Photographer, Typographer, Ausstellungskatalog Van Abbe Museum Eindhoven, 1990, S. 178 und 212 (Abb. 112)

72 El Lissitzky, The runner, Photographie, 1930, Moskau, Staatliche Tretjakov-Galerie. In: El Lissitzky: 1890-1941. Architect, Painter, Photographer, Typographer, Ausstellungskatalog Van Abbe Museum Eindhoven, 1990, S. 178 und 212 (Abb. 114)

73 László Moholy-Nagy, Projektionsphotomontage für ein Bühnenbild zu Walter Mehrings „Der Kaufmann von Berlin", Brom-Silber, Mattglanz (25,8 x 38 cm), 1929, Köln, Theatermuseum der Universität Köln. In: Schneider, Peter Paul u.a.: Literatur im Industriezeitalter. Marbacher Kataloge 42/1 und 42/2, Marbach am Neckar 1987, S. 741-744

55 George Bellows, Riverfront No. 1 (Coney Island), oil on canvas (115.3 x 236.7 cm), Columbus (Ohio), Columbus Museum of Art, 1915. In: Chwast, Seymour/Heller, Steven: The Art of New York, New York 1983, pp. 62-63

56 George Grosz, Schuhputzer (Shoe Shine Boy), drawing, 1932. In: George Grosz: New York, ed. by Walter Huder and Karl Riha, Siegen 1985

57 Miguel Covarrubias, Harlem, water colour, 1934. In: Cohen, Barbara/Chwast, Seymour/Heller, Steven: New York Observed. Artists and Writers look at the City, New York 1987, p. 91

58 Mott Street China Town, New York, photograph, 1898

59 Umberto Boccioni, Rissa in Galleria, oil on canvas (76 x 64 cm), 1910, Milan, Pinacoteca di Brera. In: Schneede, Uwe M.: Umberto Boccioni, Stuttgart 1994, p. 56 and 210

60 Berenice Abbott, Herald Square, Manhattan, photograph, 16. July 1936. In: Lloyd, Valérie: New York in the Thirties. The photographs of Berenice Abbott, Side Gallery, Newcastle-upon-Tyne 1977, cat. no. 59

61 Gustave Doré, A City Thoroughfare, wood engraving, 1872. In: Gustave Doré/Blanchard Jerrold: London. A Pilgrimage, London 1872, after p. 182

62 Gustave Doré, Ludgate Hill, wood engraving, 1872, from: Gustave Doré/Blanchard Jerrold: London. A Pilgrimage, London 1872, after p. 48

63 Werner Heldt, Berlin am Meer (Berlin by the Sea), oil on canvas (48 x 84 cm), private collection, 1952. In: Roters, Eberhard/Schulz, Bernhard: Ich und die Stadt. Mensch und Großstadt in der deutschen Kunst des 20. Jahrhunderts, exhibition catalogue Berlinische Galerie, Berlin 1987, pp. 344-345

64 Craig McPherson, Autumn, oil on canvas, 1980, New York, Museum of the City of New York. In: Chwast, Seymour/Heller, Steven: The Art of New York, New York 1983, pp. 48-49

65 Montmartre, Sunset, photograph Franziska Bollerey, April 1990

66 Neon Advertisement Bond Clothing Store, New York City, 1948-1954. Acacia Card Co., around 1950. In: Tucker, Kerry: Greetings from New York. A visit to Manhattan in Postcards, New York 1981, p. 72

67 Roof Garden of the Hotel Astor on Broadway, New York City by night. Malcolm & Hays, around 1908. In: Tucker, Kerry: Greetings from New York. A visit to Manhattan in Postcards, New York 1981, p. 74

68 Cor van Eesteren, Road Crossing in Paris, photograph, around 1925, Archive N.A.I. Rotterdam

69 Richard Matz, Weltstadtverkehr (Berlin-Alexanderplatz)(Metropolitan Traffic - Berlin Alexanderplatz), colour lithograph (67.9 x 95.9 cm), around 1933, Berlin, private collection. In: Korff, Gottfried/Rürup, Reinhard: Berlin, Berlin. Die Ausstellung zur Geschichte der Stadt, exhibition catalogue, Berlin 1987, p. 475

70 Paul Citroën, Metropolis, collage of newspaper clippings and pieces of picture postcards (76.1 x 58.4 cm), 1923. Facsimile. Photographic Archive of the Rijksuniversiteit Leiden. In: Dethier, Jean (ed.): La ville, art et architecture en Europe, 1870-1933, exhibition catalogue Centre Pompidou, Paris 1994, p. 258

71 El Lissitzky, The Runners, photo montage (12 x 21.4 cm), 1930, private collection, Gallery Berinson, Berlin. In: El Lissitzky: 1890-1941. Architect, Painter, Photographer, Typographer, exhibition catalogue Van Abbe Museum, Eindhoven, 1990, p. 178 and 212 (fig. 112)

74 John Heartfield, Schutzumschlag für Kurt Tucholsky: Deutschland, Deutschland über alles, Neuer Deutscher Verlag, Berlin 1929. In: John Heartfield. 1891-1968. Photomontages, Ausstellungskatalog Musée d'Art Moderne de la ville de Paris, Paris 1974, S. 55

75 Fotomontage (Werbung von Fox-Europa-Produktion) für den Film „Berlin. Die Sinfonie der Großstadt" (Regie: Walter Ruttmann, 1927). In: Berg Ganschow, Uta (Hrsg.): Berlin. Aussen und Innen. 53 Filme aus 90 Jahren. Stiftung deutsche Kinemathek Berlin 1984, S. 23

76 Fotomontage (Werbung von Fox-Europa-Produktion), für den Film „Berlin. Die Sinfonie der Grosßstadt" (Regie Walter Ruttmann, 1927). In: Willet, John: Explosion der Mitte. Kunst & Politik. 1917-1933, München 1981, S. 100

77 Lloyd Bacon (Regie), 42nd Street, Standbild, USA 1933

78 Walter Ruttmann (Regie), Berlin. Sinfonie der Großstadt, Standbild, Deutschland 1927

79 Walter Ruttmann (Regie), Berlin. Sinfonie der Großstadt, Standbild, Deutschland 1927

80 Erich Kettelhut, Morgendämmerung, Öl und Gouache auf Karton (39 x 54,5 cm), 1927, Entwurf für den Film Metropolis von Fritz Lang, Filmmuseum Berlin, Deutsche Kinemathek. In: Neumann, Dietrich (Hrsg.): Filmarchitektur. Von Metropolis bis Blade Runner, München/New York 1996, S. 100/101

81 Boris Bilinski, Plakat für die französische Premiere von Fritz Langs Film Metropolis, Staatliche Museen Preußischer Kulturbesitz, Kunstbibliothek Berlin. In: Neumann, Dietrich (Hrsg.): Filmarchitektur. Von Metropolis bis Blade Runner, München/New York 1996, S. 100

82 Erich Kettelhut, Stadtansicht, Öl und Gouache auf Karton für den Film „Metropolis" (Regie: Fritz Lang, 1927). In: Neumann, Dietrich (Hrsg.): Filmarchitektur. Von Metropolis bis Blade Runner, München/New York 1996, S. 97

83 Filmarchitektur nach Skizzen von Erich Kettelhut für den Film „Metropolis" (Regie: Fritz Lang, 1927). In: Berg-Ganschow, Uta und Wolfgang Jacobsen: Film...Stadt...Kino..., Ausstellungskatalog Berlin 1987, S. 94

84 David Butler (Regie), Just Imagine, Standbild, USA 1930

85 David Butler (Regie), Just Imagine, Standbild, USA 1930

86 Ridley Scott (Regie), Blade Runner, Standbild, USA 1982

87 Ridley Scott (Regie), Blade Runner, Standbild, USA 1982

88 Illustration aus: Moses Kings Views of New York. In: Moses King's Guidebook, New York 1911/12

89 Titelseite aus: Moses Kings Views of New York. In: Moses King's Guidebook, New York 1911/12

90 Hugh Ferriss: The city at night. Descent into the streets. Zeichnung. Hugh Ferriss Collection, Avery Architectural and Fine Arts Library, Columbia University New York. In: The Metropolis of Tomorrow. New York 1929, Neuauflage New York 1986. Vgl. hierzu auch: Ferriss Leich, Jean: Architectural Visions. The Drawings of Hugh Ferriss, New York 1980, S. 19

91 Hugh Ferriss: Crowding Towers. Zeichnung. Hugh Ferriss Collection, Avery Architectural and Fine Arts Library, Columbia University New York. In: The Metropolis of Tomorrow, New York 1929, Neuauflage New York 1986. Vgl. hierzu auch: Ferriss Leich, Jean: Architectural Visions. The Drawings of Hugh Ferriss New York 1980, S. 63

72 El Lissitzky, The Runner, Photography, 1930, Moscow, State Tretjakov-Gallery. In: El Lissitzky: 1890-1941. Architect, Painter, Photographer, Typographer, exhibition catalogue Van Abbe Museum, Eindhoven, 1990, p. 178 and 212 (fig. 114)

73 László Moholy-Nagy, projection photomontage for a stage design for Walter Mehring's „Der Kaufmann von Berlin", silver-bromide, matt finish (25.8 x 38 cm), 1929, Köln, Theatermuseum der Universität Köln. In: Schneider, Peter Paul et al.: Literatur im Industriezeitalter. Marbach Catalogues 42/1 and 42/2, Marbach am Neckar 1987, pp. 741-744

74 John Heartfield, dust cover for Kurt Tucholsky: Deutschland, Deutschland über alles, Neuer Deutscher Verlag, Berlin 1929. In: John Heartfield. 1891-1968. Photomontages, Exhibition catalogue Musée d'Art Moderne de la ville de Paris, Paris 1974, p. 55

75 Photomontage (Advertisement Fox-Europa-Produktion) for the film "Berlin. Die Sinfonie der Großstadt" (Director: Walter Ruttmann, 1927) In: Willet, John: Explosion der Mitte. Kunst & Politik 1917-1933, Munich 1981, p.100

76 Photomontage (Advertisement Fox-Europa-Produktion) for the film "Berlin. Die Sinfonie der Großstadt" (Director: Walter Ruttmann, 1927) In: Berg-Ganschow, Uta (ed.): Berlin. Aussen und Innen. 53 Filme aus 90 Jahren. Stiftung deutsche Kinemathek, Berlin 1984, p. 23

77 Lloyd Bacon (Director), 42nd Street, still, USA 1933

78 Walter Ruttmann (Director), Berlin. Sinfonie der Großstadt, still, Deutschland 1927

79 Walter Ruttmann (Director), Berlin. Sinfonie der Großstadt, still, Deutschland 1927

80 Erich Kettelhut, Morgendämmerung (Dawn), oil and gouache on cardboard (39 x 54.5 cm), 1927, design for the film Metropolis by Fritz Lang, Filmmuseum Berlin, Deutsche Kinemathek. In: Neumann, Dietrich (ed.): Filmarchitektur. Von Metropolis bis Blade Runner, Munich/New York 1996, pp. 100-101

81 Boris Bilinski, Poster for the French premiere of Fritz Lang's Film Metropolis, Staatliche Museen Preußischer Kulturbesitz, Kunstbibliothek Berlin, In: Neumann, Dietrich (ed.): Filmarchitektur. Von Metropolis bis Blade Runner, Munich/New York 1996, p. 100

82 Erich Kettelhut, Vision of a City, Oil and Gouache on Paper, for the Film "Metropolis" (Director: Fritz Lang, 1927). In: Neumann, Dietrich (ed.): Filmarchitektur. Von Metropolis bis Blade Runner, Munich/New York 1996, p. 97

83 Film Architecture according to the sketches of Erich Kettelhut, for the film "Metropolis" (Director: Fritz Lang, 1927). In: Berg-Ganschow, Uta/Wolfgang Jacobsen: Film… Stadt… Kino. Exhibition catalogue, Berlin 1987, p. 94

84 David Butler (Director), Just Imagine, still, USA 1930

85 David Butler (Director), Just Imagine, still, USA 1930

86 Ridley Scott (Director), Blade Runner, still, USA 1982

87 Ridley Scott (Director), Blade Runner, still, USA 1982

88 Illustration from: Moses Kings Views of New York. In: Moses King's Guidebook, New York 1911/12

89 Frontispiece from: Moses Kings Views of New York. In: Moses King's Guidebook, New York 1911/12

92 Porträt von Charles Dickens mit Szenen seiner Romane aus einer holländischen Ausgabe von David Copperfield und anderen Erzählungen, 1888. In: Tomlin, E.W.F. (Hrsg.): Charles Dickens 1812-1870. London 1969, deutsche Ausgabe, Hamburg 1969 S. 272

93 Oliver Twist, Theateraufführung, London 1905. Farblithographie einer Szene mit dem Schauspieler Beerbohm Tree als Fagin. In: Tomlin, E.W.F. (Hrsg): Charles Dickens 1812-1870, London 1969, deutsche Ausgabe Hamburg 1969, S. 173

94 Waldemar Titzenthaler, Berlin, Am Krögel, Fotografie, 1897, Berlin, Landesarchiv, Foto Nr. II 4947

95 Heinrich Zille, Frau und Kinder auf der Knobelsdorffbrücke in Charlottenburg, im Hintergrund Häuser der Sophie-Charlotte-Straße, Fotografie, um 1900, Berlin, Landesarchiv, Foto Nr. 130309

96 Käthe Kollwitz, Weihnacht. Zeichnung aus der Serie „Bilder vom Elend", Blatt VI, veröffentlicht in: Simplicissimus, 24. 01. 1910, 14. Jahrgang (1909/10). In: Hinz, Renate: Käthe Kollwitz. Druckgrafik, Plakate, Zeichnungen, Berlin 1980, S. 71

97 Käthe Kollwitz, Ins Wasser. Zeichnung aus der Serie „Bilder vom Elend", Blatt IV, veröffentlicht in: Simplicissimus, 20. 12. 1909, 14. Jahrgang (1909/10). In: Hinz, Renate: Käthe Kollwitz. Druckgrafik, Plakate, Zeichnungen, Berlin 1980, S. 69

98 Charlie Chaplin (Regie), The Kid, Standbild, USA 1921

99 Jacob A. Riis, Didn't live nowhere, Fotografie, 1890, Jacob A. Riis Collection, New York, Museum of the City of New York. In: Riis, Jacob A.: How the other half lives. Studies among the tenements of New York (1890), New York 1970, S. 157

100 Jacob A. Riis, Griechische Kinder in Gotham Court, Fotografie, 1890, Jacob A. Riis Collection, New York, Museum of the City of New York. In: Riis, Jacob A.: How the other half lives. Studies among the tenements of New York (1890), New York 1970, S. 21 und 147

101 Berenice Abbott, Talman Street, between Jay and Bridge Streets, Brooklyn, Fotografie, 1936. In: Lloyd, Valérie: New York in the Thirties. The photographs of Berenice Abbott, Side Gallery, Newcastle-upon-Tyne 1977, S. 63

102 Jacob A. Riis, N.Y. Auf dem Dach der Barracken (On the roof of the barracks), Fotografie, 1890, Jacob A. Riis Collection, New York, Museum of the City of New York. In: Riis, Jacob A.: How the other half lives. Studies among the tenements of New York (1890), New York 1970, S. 222

103 Martha Diamond, Downtown, Öl auf Leinwand (84 x 56 cm), 1981, Brooke Alexander Inc., New York City. In: Chwast, Seymour/Heller, Steven: The Art of New York, New York 1983, S. 53

104 Abraham Walkowitz, New York Abstraction, Lithographie (44,2 x 35,6 cm), 1912, Zabriskie Gallery, New York City. In: Chwast, Seymour/Heller, Steven: The Art of New York, New York 1983, S. 30

105 John Heartfield, Schutzumschlag zu Upton Sinclair: Der Sumpf, Malik Verlag Berlin 1928. In: Schneider, Peter Paul u.a.: Literatur im Industriezeitalter. Marbacher Kataloge 42/1 und 42/2, Marbach am Neckar 1987, S. 453-454

106 Ernst Aufsesser, Schutzumschlag mit Photomontage zu Bertolt Brecht: Im Dickicht der Städte. Der Kampf zweier Männer in der Riesenstadt Chicago, Propyläen Verlag, Berlin 1927. In: Schneider, Peter Paul u.a.: Literatur im Industriezeitalter. Marbacher Kataloge 42/1 und 42/2, Marbach am Neckar 1987, S. 712-714

90 Hugh Ferriss, The City at Night. Descent into the Streets. Drawing. Hugh Ferriss Collection, Avery Architectural and Fine Arts Library, Columbia University New York In: The Metropolis of Tomorrow, New York 1929, new ed. New York 1986. Cf. also: Ferriss Leich, Jean: Architectural Visions. The Drawings of Hugh Ferriss, New York 1980, p. 19

91 Hugh Ferriss, Crowding Towers. Drawing. Hugh Ferriss Collection, Avery Architectural and Fine Arts Library, Columbia University New York: The Metropolis of Tomorrow, New York 1929, new ed. New York 1986. Cf. also: Ferriss Leich, Jean: Architectural Visions. The Drawings of Hugh Ferriss, New York 1980, p. 63

92 Portrait of Charles Dickens with scenes from his novels from a Dutch edition of David Copperfield and other Stories, 1888. In: Tomlin, E.W.F. (ed.): Charles Dikkens 1812-1870. London 1969, German Edition, Hamburg 1969, p. 272

93 Oliver Twist, stage performance, London 1905, Colored lithograph of a Scene with the Actor Beerbohm Tree as Fagin: In: Tomlin, E.W.F. (ed.): Charles Dickens 1812-1870, London 1969. German Edition 1969, p. 173

94 Waldemar Titzenthaler, Berlin, Am Krögel, photograph, 1897, Berlin, Landesarchiv, photo no. II 4947

95 Heinrich Zille, Wife and Children on Knobelsdorff Bridge in Charlottenburg, in the background buildings in Sophie-Charlotte-Straße, photograph, around 1900, Berlin, Landesarchiv, photo no. 130309

96 Käthe Kollwitz, Weihnacht (Christmas). Drawing from the series "Bilder vom Elend" (Pictures of Misery), fol. VI, published in: Simplicissimus, 24. 01. 1910, 14th year (1909/10). In: Hinz, Renate: Käthe Kollwitz. Druckgrafik, Plakate, Zeichnungen, Berlin 1980, p. 71

97 Käthe Kollwitz, Ins Wasser (Into the Water). Drawing from the series "Bilder vom Elend" (Pictures of Misery), fol. IV, published in: Simplicissimus, 20. 12. 1909, 14th year (1909/10). In: Hinz, Renate: Käthe Kollwitz. Druckgrafik, Plakate, Zeichnungen, Berlin 1980, p. 69

98 Charlie Chaplin (Director), The Kid, still, USA 1921

99 Jacob A. Riis, Didn't live nowhere, photograph, 1890, Jacob A. Riis Collection, New York, Museum of the City of New York. In: Riis, Jacob A.: How the other half lives. Studies among the tenements of New York (1890), New York 1970, p. 157

100 Jacob A. Riis, Greek Children in Gotham Court, photograph, 1890, Jacob A. Riis Collection, New York, Museum of the City of New York. In: Riis, Jacob A.: How the other half lives. Studies among the tenements of New York (1890), New York 1970, p. 21 and 147

101 Berenice Abbott, Talman Street, between Jay and Bridge Streets, Brooklyn, photograph, 1936. In: Lloyd, Valérie: New York in the Thirties. The photographs of Berenice Abbott, Side Gallery, Newcastle-upon-Tyne 1977, p. 63

102 Jacob A. Riis, N.Y. Auf dem Dach der Barracken (On the roof of the sheds), photograph, 1890, Jacob A. Riis Collection, New York, Museum of the City of New York. In: Riis, Jacob A.: How the other half lives. Studies among the tenements of New York (1890), New York 1970, p. 222

103 Martha Diamond, Downtown, oil on canvas (84 x 56 cm), 1981, Brooke Alexander Inc., New York City. In: Chwast, Seymour/Heller, Steven: The Art of New York, New York 1983, p. 53

107 Schutzumschlag zu Paul Grulich: Dämon Berlin. Aufzeichnungen eines Obdachlosen, Berlin 1907. In: Korff, Gottfried/Rürup, Reinhard: Berlin, Berlin. Die Ausstellung zur Geschichte der Stadt, Ausstellungskatalog, Berlin 1987, S. 315

108 Chicago von der Aussichtsterrasse des Hancock Center, Fotografie Axel Föhl, Juli 1990

109 Martin Weinberg, Schutzumschlag zu Seitz, Robert/Zucker, Heinz (Hrsg.): Um uns die Stadt. Eine Anthologie neuer Großstadtdichtung, Sieben-Stäbe-Verlag, Berlin 1931

110 Schutzumschlag zu Roters, Eberhard/Schulz, Bernhard (Hrsg.): Ich und die Stadt. Mensch und Großstadt in der deutschen Kunst des 20. Jahrhunderts, Berlin 1987

111 Ludwig Meidner, Ich und die Stadt, Öl auf Leinwand (60 x 50 cm), 1913, Privatbesitz. In: Korff, Gottfried/Rürup, Reinhard: Berlin, Berlin. Die Ausstellung zur Geschichte der Stadt, Ausstellungskatalog, Berlin 1987, S. 88

112 UMBO (Otto Umbehr). Der rasende Reporter, Egon Erwin Kisch, Photocollage, 1926. In: Umbo. Vom Bauhaus zum Bildjournalismus. Ausstellungskatalog Düsseldorf (Kunstverein für die Rheinlande und Westfalen) 1995, Katalognummer 23

113 John Heartfield, Es kommt darauf an, wohin die Reise geht, Photomontage, um 1927. In: John Heartfield. 1891-1986. fotomontages. Ausstellungskatalog Paris, Musée d'Art Moderne Ein Gespenst geht um in Europa, 1927

114 Herbert Bayer, Einsamer Großstädter/Selbstporträt, Fotomontage, 1932. In: Herbert Bayer. Das künstlerische Werk 1918-1938, Ausstellungskatalog Bauhaus-Archiv, Berlin 1982, S. 12

115 Ernst Ludwig Kirchner, Brandenburger Tor, Öl auf Leinwand (120 x 150 cm), 1929, Berlin, Staatliche Museen Preußischer Kulturbesitz, Nationalgalerie. In: Ernst Ludwig Kirchner, Ausstellungskatalog Nationalgalerie Berlin, Berlin 1980, S. 381

116 George Grosz, Grauer Tag, Öl auf Leinwand (115 x 80 cm), 1921, Berlin, Staatliche Museen Preußischer Kulturbesitz, Nationalgalerie. In: Roters, Eberhard/Schulz, Bernhard: Ich und die Stadt. Mensch und Großstadt in der deutschen Kunst des 20. Jahrhunderts, Ausstellungskatalog Berlinische Galerie, Berlin 1987, S. 390-391

117 Rudolf Schlichter, Hausvogteiplatz, Aquarell (66,5 x 51,5 cm), Offenbach, Galerie Volker Huber, 1926. In: Roters, Eberhard/Schulz, Bernhard: Ich und die Stadt. Mensch und Großstadt in der deutschen Kunst des 20. Jahrhunderts, Ausstellungskatalog Berlinische Galerie, Berlin 1987, S. 174-175

118 George Grosz, Straßenszene, Aquarellierte Federzeichnung (58,4 x 46 cm), 1923, Privatbesitz. In: Roters, Eberhard/Schulz, Bernhard: Ich und die Stadt. Mensch und Großstadt in der deutschen Kunst des 20. Jahrhunderts, Ausstellungskatalog Berlinische Galerie, Berlin 1987, S. 198-199

119 George Grosz, Stützen der Gesellschaft, Öl auf Leinwand, (200 x 108 cm), 1926. Staatliche Museen Preussischer Kulturbesitz, Nationalgalerie. In: Berlin (Inv. Nr. NG 4/58) In: Schuster, Peter-Klaus: Georg Grosz. Berlin-New York. Ausstellungskatalog Nationalgalerie Berlin, 1994/95, S. 347

120 Ernst Ludwig Kirchner, Drei Straßenmädchen vor Schaufenster, Pastell (55,8 x 35,9 cm), 1914, Stuttgart, Staatsgalerie. In: Roters, Eberhard/Schulz, Bernhard: Ich und die Stadt. Mensch und Großstadt in der deutschen Kunst des 20. Jahrhunderts, Ausstellungskatalog Berlinische Galerie, Berlin 1987, S. 70-71

104 Abraham Walkowitz, New York Abstraction, lithograph (44.2 x 35.6 cm), 1912, Zabriskie Gallery, New York City. In: Chwast, Seymour/Heller, Steven: The Art of New York, New York 1983, p. 30

105 John Heartfield, dust cover for Upton Sinclair: Der Sumpf, Malik Verlag Berlin 1928. In: Schneider, Peter Paul et al.: Literatur im Industriezeitalter. Marbacher Kataloge 42/1 and 42/2, Marbach am Neckar 1987, pp. 453-454

106 Ernst Aufsesser, dust cover with photomontage for Bertolt Brecht: Im Dickicht der Städte. Der Kampf zweier Männer in der Riesenstadt Chicago, Propyläen Verlag, Berlin 1927. In: Schneider, Peter Paul et al.: Literatur im Industriezeitalter. Marbacher Kataloge 42/1 and 42/2, Marbach am Neckar 1987, p. 712-714

107 Dust cover for Paul Grulich: Dämon Berlin. Aufzeichnungen eines Obdachlosen, Berlin 1907. In: Korff, Gottfried/ Rürup, Reinhard: Berlin, Berlin. Die Ausstellung zur Geschichte der Stadt, exhibition catalogue, Berlin 1987, p. 315

108 Chicago from the viewing platform of the Hancock Center, photograph Axel Föhl, July 1990

109 Martin Weinberg, dust cover for Seitz, Robert/Zucker, Heinz (ed.): Um uns die Stadt. Eine Anthologie neuer Großstadtdichtung, Sieben-Stäbe-Verlag, Berlin 1931

110 Dust cover for Roters, Eberhard/ Schulz, Bernhard (ed.): Ich und die Stadt. Mensch und Großstadt in der deutschen Kunst des 20. Jahrhunderts, Exhibition catalogue Berlinische Galerie, Berlin 1987

111 Ludwig Meidner, Ich und die Stadt, oil on canvas (60 x 50 cm), 1913, private collection. In: Korff, Gottfried/Rürup, Reinhard: Berlin, Berlin. Die Ausstellung zur Geschichte der Stadt, exhibition catalogue, Berlin 1987, p. 88

112 UMBO (Otto Umbehr). Der rasende Reporter (The Speeding Reporter), Egon Erwin Kisch, photocollage, 1926. In: Umbo. Vom Bauhaus zum Bildjournalismus. Exhibition catalogue Kunstverein für die Rheinlande und Westfalen, Düsseldorf 1995, cat. no. 23

113 John Heartfield, Es kommt darauf an, wohin die Reise geht (It depends on where the journey is going to), photomontage, around 1927. In: John Heartfield. 1891-1986. Photomontages. Exhibition catalogue, Musée d'Art Moderne, Paris. Ein Gespenst geht um in Europa, Photomontage, 1927

114 Herbert Bayer, Einsamer Großstädter/Selbstbildnis (Lonely Urban Citizen/ Self Portrait), photomontage, 1932. In: Herbert Bayer. Das künstlerische Werk 1918-1938, exhibition catalogue Bauhaus-Archive, Berlin 1982, p. 12

115 Ernst Ludwig Kirchner, Brandenburger Tor, oil on canvas (120 x 150 cm), 1929, Berlin, Staatliche Museen Preußischer Kulturbesitz, Nationalgalerie. In: Ernst Ludwig Kirchner, exhibition catalogue Nationalgalerie Berlin, Berlin 1980, p. 381

116 George Grosz, Grauer Tag, oil on canvas (115 x 80 cm), 1921, Berlin, Staatliche Museen Preußischer Kulturbesitz, Nationalgalerie. In: Roters, Eberhard/Schulz, Bernhard: Ich und die Stadt. Mensch und Großstadt in der deutschen Kunst des 20. Jahrhunderts, exhibition catalogue Berlinische Galerie, Berlin 1987, pp. 390-391

117 Rudolf Schlichter, Hausvogteiplatz, watercolour (66.5 x 51.5 cm), Offenbach, Galerie Volker Huber, 1926. In: Roters, Eberhard/Schulz, Bernhard: Ich und die Stadt. Mensch und Großstadt in der deutschen Kunst des 20. Jahrhunderts, Exhibition catalogue Berlinische Galerie, Berlin 1987, pp. 174-175

121 Ernst Ludwig Kirchner, Berliner Straßenszene, Öl auf Leinwand (121 x 95 cm), 1913, Berlin, Brücke-Museum. In: Roters, Eberhard/Schulz, Bernhard: Ich und die Stadt. Mensch und Großstadt in der deutschen Kunst des 20. Jahrhunderts, Ausstellungskatalog Berlinische Galerie, Berlin 1987, S. 62-63

122 Richard Ziegler, Vor dem Schaufenster, Pastell auf Japanbütten (37 x 28 cm), Calw, Richard-Ziegler-Stiftung, 1927/28. In: Korff, Gottfried/Rürup, Reinhard: Berlin, Berlin. Die Ausstellung zur Geschichte der Stadt, Ausstellungskatalog, Berlin 1987, S. 492, 495

123 Marc Chagall, Vision von Paris, Farblithographie (32 x 24,5 cm), 1960. In: Marc Chagall. Bonjour Paris. 23 Lithographien mit einer Einführung von Wolf Stadler, Freiburg im Breisgau 1983, S. 35

124 Marc Chagall, Paris bei Nacht, Farblithographie (38 x 28cm), 1954. In: Marc Chagall. Bonjour Paris. 23 Lithographien mit einer Einführung von Wolf Stadler, Freiburg im Breisgau 1983, S. 6

125 Buchtitel unter Verwendung einer Lithographie (Straßenszene) von Fernand Léger von 1954. In: Blaise Cendrars/ Fernand Léger: Paris. Ma Ville. Paris 1987, S. 71

126 Fernand Léger, Gare, Lithographie. In: Blaise Cendrars/Fernand Léger: Paris. Ma Ville (1954-57). Paris 1987 und München 1987, S. 61

127 ter Hell, Ich bin's, Mischtechnik auf Leinwand (260 x 308 cm), Berlin, Berlinische Galerie, 1980. In: Roters, Eberhard/Schulz, Bernhard: Ich und die Stadt. Mensch und Großstadt in der deutschen Kunst des 20. Jahrhunderts, Ausstellungskatalog Berlinische Galerie, Berlin 1987, S. 390-391

128 Die Stadt kennen lernen (Learning about the city) Fotografie, 1899 von Frances Benjamin Johnston (Library of Congress). In: Gutheim, Frederick/Wilcomb E. Washburn: The Federal City. Plans and Realities. Smithonian Institution, Washington D.C., 1976, S. 33, Abb. 15

118 George Grosz, Straßenszene (Street Scene), ink drawing with watercolour (58.4 x 46 cm), 1923, private collection. In: Roters, Eberhard/Schulz, Bernhard: Ich und die Stadt. Mensch und Großstadt in der deutschen Kunst des 20. Jahrhunderts, exhibition catalogue Berlinische Galerie, Berlin 1987, pp. 198-199

119 George Grosz, Pillars of Society, oil on canvas (200 x 108 cm), 1926. Berlin, Staatliche Museen Preussischer Kulturbesitz, Nationalgalerie, 1926 (Inv. No. NG 4/58). In: Schuster, Peter-Klaus: George Grosz. Berlin-New York. Exhibition catalogue, Nationalgalerie Berlin 1994/95, p. 347

120 Ernst Ludwig Kirchner, Drei Straßenmädchen vor Schaufenster (Three Street Girls in front of a Shop Window), pastel (55.8 x 35.9 cm), 1914, Stuttgart, Staatsgalerie. In: Roters, Eberhard/Schulz, Bernhard: Ich und die Stadt. Mensch und Großstadt in der deutschen Kunst des 20. Jahrhunderts. Exhibition catalogue Berlinische Galerie, Berlin 1987, pp. 70-71

121 Ernst Ludwig Kirchner, Berliner Straßenszene (Berlin Street Scene), oil on canvas (121 x 95 cm), 1913, Berlin, Brücke-Museum. In: Roters, Eberhard/Schulz, Bernhard: Ich und die Stadt. Mensch und Großstadt in der deutschen Kunst des 20. Jahrhunderts, exhibition catalogue Berlinische Galerie, Berlin 1987, p. 62-63

122 Richard Ziegler, Vor dem Schaufenster, pastel on laid paper (37 x 28 cm), Calw, Richard-Ziegler-Stiftung, 1927/28. In: Korff, Gottfried/Rürup, Reinhard: Berlin, Berlin. Die Ausstellung zur Geschichte der Stadt, exhibition catalogue, Berlin 1987, p. 492, 495

123 Marc Chagall, Vision of Paris, Colored Lithography (32 x 24.5 cm), 1960. In: Marc Chagall: Bonjour Paris. 23 Litographien mit einer Einführung von Wolf Stadler, Freiburg im Breisgau 1983, p. 35

124 Marc Chagall, Paris by Night, Colored Lithography: (38 x 28 cm), 1954. In: Bonjour Paris. 23 Litographien mit einer Einführung von Wolf Stadler, Freiburg im Breisgau 1983, p. 6

125 Book Cover with a lithograph (street scene) by Fernand Léger of 1954. In: Blaise Cendrars/Fernand Léger: Paris. Ma Ville (1954-57), Paris 1987 and Munich 1987, p. 71

126 Fernand Léger, Gare, lithograph. In: Blaise Cendrars/Fernand Léger: Paris. Ma Ville. Paris 1987, p. 61

127 ter Hell, Ich bin's (Its Me), mixed technique on canvas (260 x 308 cm), Berlin, Berlinische Galerie, 1980. In: Roters, Eberhard/Schulz, Bernhard: Ich und die Stadt. Mensch und Großstadt in der deutschen Kunst des 20. Jahrhunderts, exhibition catalogue Berlinische Galerie, Berlin 1987, pp. 390-391

128 Learning about the city, 1899. Photograph Frances Benjamin Johnston (Library of Congress). In: Gutheim, Frederick/Wilcomb E. Washburn: The Federal City. Plans and Realities. Smithonian Institution, Washington D.C., 1976, p. 33, illus. 15

Bildnachweis / Photo Credits

Franziska Bollerey: 1, 2, 6, 8, 9, 10, 15-22, 25-27, 29, 30, 35, 37-41, 65, 108; Berlin, Eulenspiegel Verlag: 14; Berlin, Filmmuseum Berlin, Deutsche Kinemathek: 80; Berlin, Landesarchiv: 23, 24, 94, 95; Berlin, Staatliche Museen Preußischer Kulturbesitz, Kunstbibliothek: 81; Berlin, Staatliche Museen Preußischer Kulturbesitz, Neue Nationalgalerie: 47; Berlin, Stiftung Stadtmuseum: 28, 33; Boston, Museum of Fine Arts: 54; Calw, Richard-Ziegler-Stiftung: 122; Columbus (Ohio), Columbus Museum of Art: 55; The Heartfield Community of Heirs / VG Bild-Kunst, Bonn 2005: 113; Mailand, Pinacoteca di Brera: 59; München, Prestel: 82; München, Schirmer-Mosel: 52; New York, Kennedy-Galleries: 53; New York, Museum of Modern Art: 4; Offenbach, Galerie Volker Huber: 117; Oggebbio (VB) Italien, The Oskar Schlemmer Estate and Archive, 49, 50; Ostfildern, Falk-Verlag: 5; Wichtrach/Bern, Ingeborg & Dr. Wolfgang Henze-Ketterer: 115, 120, 121; Siegen, Machwerk-Verlag: 13; Rotterdam, N.A.I., Archiv: 68; Stuttgart/Leipzig, Reclam: 11; VG Bild-Kunst, Bonn 2009: 12, 34, 36, 48, 56, 63, 70, 71, 72, 73, 114, 116, 118, 119, 123-126; Zürich, Archithese: 3

Leider konnten trotz intensiver Bemühungen nicht bei sämtlichen Bildern die Inhaber der Urheberrechte ermittelt werden. Diese werden gegebenenfalls gebeten, sich mit dem Verlag in Verbindung zu setzen.

Unfortunately we were unable to identify all copyright holders of the pictures. If applicable, we would ask them to please contact the publisher.

Bibliografische Information Der Deutschen Nationalbibliothek
Die Deutsche Nationalbibliothek verzeichnet diese Publikation in der Deutschen Nationalbibliografie; detaillierte bibliografische Daten sind im Internet über
< http://dnb.d-nb.de > abrufbar.

Impressum / Imprint

2., überarbeitete Auflage 2010

www.gebrmannverlag.de

Gestaltung und Umschlag: Catharina van Esch
Übersetzung: Axel Föhl & Kerstin Hall
Typoscript: Lida van Tongeren
Litho: Sieca Repro, Delft
Druck: DZA Druckerei zu Altenburg GmbH, Altenburg

Vorsatzblatt: Collage unter Verwendung einer Projektionsfotomontage
von László Moholy-Nagy für ein Bühnenbild zu Walter Mehrings „Der Kaufmann von Berlin“, 1929

Gedruckt auf säurefreiem Papier, das die US-ANSI-NORM über Haltbarkeit erfüllt.

Printed in Germany · ISBN 978-3-7861-2594-5

VICTOR
BRÄUTE-
VERTRIEBS-
A.G.